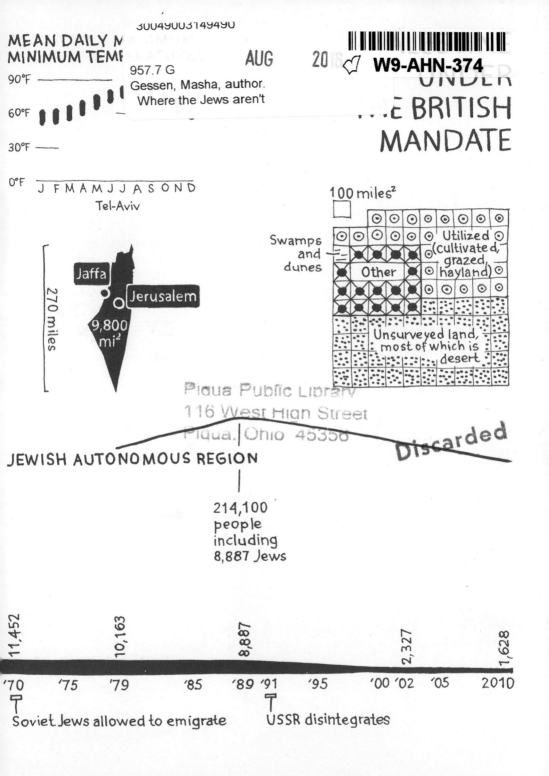

JEWISH ENCOUNTERS

Jewish Encounters is a collaboration between Schocken and Nextbook, a project devoted to the promotion of Jewish literature, culture, and ideas.

>nextbook

PUBLISHED

THE LIFE OF DAVID · Robert Pinsky

MAIMONIDES · Sherwin B. Nuland

BARNEY ROSS · Douglas Century

BETRAYING SPINOZA · Rebecca Goldstein

EMMA LAZARUS · Esther Schor

THE WICKED SON · David Mamet

MARC CHAGALL · Jonathan Wilson

JEWS AND POWER · Ruth R. Wisse

BENJAMIN DISRAELI · Adam Kirsch

RESURRECTING HEBREW · Ilan Stavans

THE JEWISH BODY · Melvin Konner

RASHI · Elie Wiesel

A FINE ROMANCE · David Lehman

YEHUDA HALEVI · Hillel Halkin

HILLEL · Joseph Telushkin

BURNT BOOKS · Rodger Kamenetz

THE EICHMANN TRIAL · Deborah E. Lipstadt

SACRED TRASH · Adina Hoffman and Peter Cole

BEN-GURION · Shimon Peres with David Landau

WHEN GENERAL GRANT EXPELLED THE JEWS · Jonathan D. Sarna

THE BOOK OF JOB · Harold S. Kushner

THE WORLDS OF SHOLEM ALEICHEM · Jeremy Dauber

THE RISE OF ABRAHAM CAHAN · Seth Lipsky

MENACHEM BEGIN · Daniel Gordis

ABRAHAM · Alan M. Dershowitz

WHERE THE JEWS AREN'T · Masha Gessen

FORTHCOMING

JUDAH MACCABEE · Jeffrey Goldberg
THE DAIRY RESTAURANT · Ben Katchor
FROM PASHAS TO PARIAHS · Lucette Lagnado
YOUR SHOW OF SHOWS · David Margolick
MRS. FREUD · Daphne Merkin
MESSIANISM · Leon Wieseltier

Where the Jews Aren't

MASHA GESSEN

WHERE THE JEWS AREN'T

The Sad and Absurd Story of Birobidzhan,
Russia's Jewish Autonomous Region

NEXTBOOK · SCHOCKEN · NEW YORK

Library of Congress Cataloging-in-Publication Data
Names: Gessen, Masha, author.
Title: Where the Jews aren't : the sad and absurd story of Birobidzhan,
    Russia's Jewish autonomous region / Masha Gessen.
Description: First edition. New York : Nextbook/Schocken [2016]
Series: Jewish encounters series. Includes bibliographical references.
Identifiers: LCCN 2015049370 (print). LCCN 2015050024 (ebook).
    ISBN 9780805242461 (hardback). ISBN 9780805243413 (ebook).
Subjects: LCSH: Birobidzhan (Russia)—History. Evreæiskaëiìa
    avtonomnaëiìa oblasti (Russia)—History. Jews—Russia (Federation)—
    Birobidzhan. BISAC: HISTORY/Europe/Former Soviet Republics.
    HISTORY/Jewish. BIOGRAPHY & AUTOBIOGRAPHY/Literary.
Classification: LCC DK771.B5 G47 2016 (print). LCC DK771.B5 (ebook).
    DDC 957/.7—dc23
LC record available at: lccn.loc.gov/2015049370

www.schocken.com

Jacket illustration: Poster produced in the Soviet Union in 1929 by OZET
(Organization of Jewish Land Workers) to advertise a fund-raising lottery
to support Jewish migration to Birobidzhan. Text, from top to bottom:
"We will finish with the old more quickly if we participate in the OZET
lottery." "Every OZET lottery ticket bought will increase the number of
Jewish agricultural laborers." "To the green news shoots of the laboring
fields." Photograph of poster by Buyenlarge / Getty Images.
Jacket design by Kelly Blair
Infographic on endpapers and map on page 2 by Darya Oreshkina.

Printed in the United States of America
First Edition
2 4 6 8 9 7 5 3 1

To my parents, who had the courage to emigrate

And thus have I been sitting for so long at the gate of this city, into which no one enters and from which no one leaves.

Everything I once knew I have now long forgotten, and in this mind of mine nothing more than a single thought remains:

All, all have long since died, and I alone am alive, and no longer await anyone.

And when I look above me once more, and feel the power and might that sleep in me, I no longer even sigh, but simply think:

I am the guardian of a dead city.

—DAVID BERGELSON,
Nokh Alemen (When All Is Said and Done)

Where the Jews Aren't

PROLOGUE

At the age of twelve I sat on the floor and had what felt like the most important conversation of my life with my best friend, who was mostly silent. I sat on the floor because I had been ambushed by puberty and now towered over my friend when standing. He was the other Jewish kid on the block, so we had been inseparable for years. There used to be two other Jewish children our age living one block over, in another nine-story, twelve-entrance concrete apartment monolith. One of those kids had disappeared about a year earlier, and his friend, the other one, told us in a hushed, serious voice that the kid had emigrated to Israel.

I sat on the floor because doing so underscored the dramatic bareness of the room. The apartment had felt desolate and barely inhabited for the last six months, since my parents had shipped all our books to America. After filing our exit-visa application with the appropriate authorities, they had spent night after night at the kitchen table poring over two different world atlases, letters from friends who had emigrated long ago, and assorted magazines—choosing their destination, under the yellow light of a kitchen lamp, in the dark. Except for one recent trip to Poland, they had never been outside the Soviet Union; the world seemed too large and too silent for them to make a choice. Finally, citing friends, purported job opportunities, and a familiar climate, they settled on Boston—and shipped all our books there.

"This is crazy," I said to my best friend. "Why leave one place where Jews are in a minority, only to go to another?" He listened uncomfortably. His parents had opted to stay in the Soviet Union. This choice had opened a chasm between us. My friend and I, our parents, the parents of the kids from the other block, all of our extended families going back for centuries—our people—had been engaged in an ongoing argument. When should the Jews stay put and when should the Jews run? How do we know where we will be safe? Does departure ever signal cowardice? Can the failure to leave be a betrayal of life itself? There is only one right answer to any given question at any given time. If you get it wrong, you may pay with your life.

Before applying for an exit visa, my parents had spent six years arguing about emigration—in the way in which they argued: my mother cajoled my father, reasoned with him, and screamed at him, and he played stone stubborn. My mother argued that it was necessary for my future: if we stayed in the Soviet Union, I would not be admitted to university. In their preoccupation with my imaginary college career in the United States or the USSR, my parents were oblivious to the fact that in grade school I had been beaten almost daily for being Jewish and in middle school I was ostracized and feared, because I had learned to fight back. When I was eight, my brother was born and my parents turned to arguing about whether they had to emigrate for both of our futures. In 1978, when my brother was three and I was eleven, they made the call—and we all finally landed on one side of the debate. From here, the people who were staying looked lost. But I thought my parents were acting foolhardily, too: I was sure that the only place we could be safe was Israel.

I talked about this with my best friend and with my parents and with the friends I saw on Saturday nights in front of the synagogue in central Moscow. That was an unofficial Jewish youth hangout: we moved around in clumps, exchanging news and rumors on the state of everyone's exit-visa application, then broke off to go to someone's house to sit around singing Yiddish and Hebrew songs. Once, following a Simchat Torah celebration in front of the synagogue—it was the one night of the year when we sang out in the street, in plain view of the police—I ran into the mother of the remaining Jewish boy from one block over. She and I took the subway home together, and on the way I talked to her about this.

Our conversation hovered over a very limited range of choices. There was the possibility of staying in the Soviet Union, an option that my parents had taught me to believe was irresponsible and immoral. We lived in a country where we were hated. Throughout my childhood, this hatred assumed the relatively benign form of consistent discrimination: Jews faced extreme hurdles gaining admission to universities and obtaining jobs; the study of Hebrew and most forms of Jewish communal life were criminalized. Who could tell when this daily hatred would again turn deadly for the Jews? There was the Israel option, which, for lack of any reliable information about that country—and in the presence of unrelenting anti-Zionist propaganda in the Soviet papers—was reserved for those brave enough to face utter uncertainty in the name of the cause. I believed myself to be one of these people, but my parents had other plans. There were the countries of the New World—the United States, Australia, and Canada—which granted asylum to Soviet Jews with relative ease and were considered an option for those who were not so idealistic as they were enterprising. My parents, two exceedingly shy intellectuals in their mid-thirties, were trying on this role. And then there was the Old World, whose geographic proximity and cultural luster made it the object of our dreams, but it was, as ever, off-limits: the countries of Western Europe were not giving out visas to Jews fleeing Russia.

Just two generations earlier—indeed, even a generation earlier, just after the Second World War—this conversation would have included one more option, one that had now receded to something between fantasy and a joke. Time was, it was spoken of with the same breathless hope with which my friends and I now spoke about Israel or Paris; it had seemed, to some, as logical a solution to the Jewish question as the United States or Canada. The place was called Birobidzhan. Founded in the 1930s, it was perhaps the worst good idea ever. It was born, as such ideas are, of a rational premise. It was, as such ideas are, deceptively simple. Why dream of a Jewish state? the logic went. Why conjure up utopias of inaccessible places, restored languages, of Jews creating their own military? All the Jews really need, according to this thinking, is to be left alone, with their language and their culture, in the confines of their own home. A home should be familiar and well protected—best when it is protected by the might and authority of an established state. The Soviet Union had taken the logic of autonomism—I wouldn't learn that word for another several decades—and turned it into a haven and a nightmare.

At twelve, I knew nothing of autonomism, but I had an instinctive understanding of the argument—and a stubborn fixation on its radical opposite, Israel. "They might as well drag us to Birobidzhan," I said bitterly, and this served, among other things, to dissipate the tension, allowing my best friend to relax slightly. For us, at the tail end of the 1970s, Birobidzhan was a comic aside to the conversation.

What did I know of it? One of my grandmothers, an inveterate traveler, had once brought home a Birobidzhan newspaper, picked up during a journey to the Soviet Far East. The newspaper was in indecipherable script, and my great-grandmother, the last surviving shtetl Jew in the family, identified the language as Yiddish. The study of Hebrew was illegal in the Soviet Union, and a newspaper that used the ancient Jewish alphabet (but was not in Hebrew) held, to me, the flavor of both a forbidden fruit and a mockery, very much like the land from which it came. I examined the newspaper closely, repeatedly, and fruitlessly, since I would never be able to learn what it said. I tried to imagine who might be in the business of printing a Yiddish-language newspaper in some faraway city, somewhere beyond Siberia. Were they young Jews like my friends and me? Some of us took Hebrew lessons, though my parents forbade me to, because they feared the teacher was an agent provocateur. Did any of them secretly rearrange the letters to make Hebrew words? Or were they men and women of my great-grandmother's generation, urbanized Yiddish speakers from the shtetlach? My great-grandmother considered Yiddish to be something less than a language; she referred to it, with evident condescension, as "the jargon." Or were they the Jews from Sholem Aleichem's stories, preserved in their shtetl ways as miraculously as the language itself?

They were all of it, and they were nothing I could imagine. They were indeed urbanized former shtetl Jews, and they had indeed miraculously preserved some of the old ways. The people who put out the Birobidzhan Yiddish paper were old men (and one woman) then, but in their youth, in the 1930s, they had been very much like my friends and me, convinced that their mission in life was to find and secure the one place in the world that would make a true home for the Jews. They had been just as righteous, just as scared, and just as hopeful as we, the crowd of similarly overliterate and underinformed young people who gathered in front of the synagogue on Saturday nights. Half a century earlier, they had traveled to the end of the earth to build that home, and the story of the dissolution of their dream, in its cruel absurdity, can be read as the quintessence of the story of Jews in Russia.

It was a story no one could tell me when I was a child. The story of Russian Jewry had been told in English, by American Jews; to them, it was a story that began with antiquity, culminated with the pogroms, and ended with emigration. For those who remained in Russia, there had been a time before the pogroms and a time after: a period of hope, then a period of fear and even greater fear and then brief hope again, and then a different kind of fear, when one no longer feared for one's life but feared never having hope again. This story did not end; it faded into a picture of my parents sitting at the kitchen table poring over an atlas of the world, or of me sitting on the bedroom floor talking at my best friend.

The history of the Soviet Union itself remains a story without a narrative; every attempt to tell this story in Russia has stopped short, giving way to the resolve to turn away from the decades of pain and suffering and bloodshed. With every telling, stories of Stalinism and the Second World War become more mythologized. And with so few Jews left in Russia, with so little uniting them, the Russian Jewish world is one of absences and silences.

I had no words for this when I was twelve, but what I felt more strongly than anything, more strongly even than the desire to go to Israel, was this absence of a story. My Jewishness consisted of the experience of being ostracized and beaten up and the specter of not being allowed into university. Once I found my people milling outside the synagogue (we never went inside, where old men in strange clothes sang in an unfamiliar language), a few old Yiddish songs and a couple of newer Hebrew ones were added to my non-story. Finally, I had read the stories of Sholem Aleichem, which were certainly of a different world, as distant from my modern urban Russian-speaking childhood as anything could be. In the end, my Jewish identity was entirely negative: it consisted of non-belonging.

How had I and other late-Soviet Jews been so impoverished? Prior to the Russian Revolution, most of the world's Jews lived in the Russian Empire. Following the Second World War, Russia was the only European country whose Jewish population numbered not in the hundreds or even thousands but in the millions. How did this country rid itself of Jewish culture altogether? How did the Jews of Russia lose their home? Much later, as I tried to find the answers to these questions, I kept circling back to the story of Birobidzhan, which, in its concentrated tragic absurdity, seemed to tell it all.

The Bolshevik state, born in October 1917, was to be international in spirit and national in structure. The Russian Empire would be reconstituted as a federation of national autonomies—a Jewish autonomy, one among many, for the Jews, after centuries of discrimination and decades of pogroms, would finally be treated like any other ethnic group. After a series of false starts, ground for the Jewish Autonomous Region was broken in the Far East, near the border with China.

Over the next eighty years, Birobidzhan would hold a cracked and crooked mirror up to the story of the Jews in Russia. Anti-Semitic purges would be magnified; gains in Jewish identity fostered by the formation and persistence of Israel would be minimized. In the end, Birobidzhan would be, nominally, one of the world's two Jewish states—the one where the Jews did not live. It would go through all the stages of failed statebuilding: from hope to hardship to pain and fear to loss and emptiness, until it seemed, finally, ridiculous. It would be a place with a Yiddish-language newspaper and no Yiddish-speaking residents.

In the late 1920s and early 1930s, tens of thousands of Jews moved to

Birobidzhan, chased from the shtetlach by poverty, hunger, and fear. They were enticed to come, greeted upon arrival, and written about breathlessly by a small group of intellectuals who envisioned building a country like no other: a home forged by the Jews for the Jews, a place where the Jews worked the land, a place where the Jews had nothing to fear but the cruel climate and the Siberian tiger. They envisioned turning Yiddish, the "jargon" of their households, into the universal language of secular Judaism, the language of literature, theater, and education that would form the basis of a twentieth-century, post-oppression Jewish culture. What had been the language of Jewish poverty was to become the language of their poetry, and half a dozen young poets toiled to make it so. In the 1930s, Yiddish was, briefly, the unofficial state language of Birobidzhan. The short period of state-building ended in the mid-1930s with arrests and purges of the Communist Party and the cultural elite. The Yiddish theater was shut down; the young Yiddish poets were de-published. The Birobidzhan project went silent.

Hope, crippled by tragedy but still alive, reasserted itself in Birobidzhan after the Second World War, when the Jewish Autonomous Region, as it was now called, received a new influx of Jews. Once again, these were the hungry, the maimed, and the dispossessed from what had once been the Pale of Settlement, the part of the Russian Empire where Jews could legally settle. Most of them had lost their families in the Holocaust. They had no one and no place to return to. If they held any hope for building a home in Birobidzhan, it was hope of the desperate sort.

Another wave of arrests swept through Birobidzhan in the late 1940s, taking the middle-aged Yiddish-language poets to prison and frightening the rest of the Jews into silence. The poets returned to Birobidzhan almost ten years later, frail old men (and one woman). It was they who, in the late 1970s, were publishing the Soviet Union's only Yiddish-language newspaper. Their readership was dwindling by the day as the last of Europe's Yiddish speakers were dying of old age in the center of Asia. Most of them were still too frightened to speak Yiddish in public, or to tell their children that being Jewish had once meant something.

As the last of the poets died, in the late 1980s, the memory of the dream that never came to be in Birobidzhan lived on only in their writing—and in the memory of a man who had been the one young editor at the Birobidzhan newspaper back when I, a preteen in Moscow, was staring at the printed words in Yiddish. The man, it seems, was the sole young person in Birobidzhan who wanted to find out what dream it was he was supposed to be living. The only son of a war widow, he had taught himself Yiddish at the age of seventeen, becoming one of the youngest people in his part of the world to speak the dying language.

The man lives in Jerusalem now; he left Russia in 1990, chased by the ghost of his ancestors' dreams. My childhood best friend left Russia around the same time; he currently divides his time between New York and Tokyo. Not even the Hebrew teacher whom my parents suspected of being a KGB agent provocateur lives in Moscow now: he was granted his exit visa around the same time as my family, and he moved to Boston—as did we. I myself spent time in Israel but never stayed; I lived in the United States until I was in my mid-twenties, then returned to Moscow—first as an American reporter, an outsider, but gradually turning native again. When I wrote the first draft of this book, in 2010, I was raising two children in Russia, a country whose Jewish culture had been virtually erased, and on occasion I wondered if I was making a mistake. The virulent anti-Semitism I remembered from my childhood was gone, but occasionally a relatively harmless expression of it would make me wonder just how far below the surface the danger had gone, and I felt the fear creeping up in me. The questions of the generations of Jews before me, including my parents, came back to haunt me. When should the Jews stay put and when should the Jews run? How do we know where we will be safe? Does departure ever signal cowardice? Can the failure to leave be a betrayal of life itself? There is only one right answer to any given question at any given time, and how can I tell when the time has come to know the difference?

At twelve, I longed desperately to know where my true home might be. Thirty years later, I was apparently free to choose my own destination, and far better versed in the physical ways of the world. Yet I remained suspended in mistrust, hedging my geographical bets like so many generations of Jews before me. In part in an attempt to understand or at least describe this state, I set out to write a book about Birobidzhan.

In December 2013, I found myself sitting on the floor in the study of my Moscow apartment. The room was nearly empty, the bookshelves were barren, and the last of the guests at our going-away party were still drinking in the kitchen, even after my partner and two of our three kids had gone to sleep on the one remaining mattress on the floor in our bedroom. Our plane to New York would leave in a few hours. Just months earlier, we had decided that it was time to run; waiting any longer would put our family in danger. This time, the choice did not have to do with being Jewish: the Kremlin had unleashed a campaign against gays, and my partner and I happened to be that, too. The parliament was discussing ways to remove children from LGBT families. The threat seemed alternately far-fetched and immediate, but the risk, we decided, was unacceptable in either case.

I sat on the floor, hoping that my absence from the living room would compel the stragglers to leave. I looked down at the molding, where the wall met the floor—it was painted light blue, and the radiator was dark blue, and this had been done in accordance with my sketches. The tears came then, and this was the first time in my life's many moves—from the Soviet Union to the United States, then back to Russia, now back to America—that I cried for what had been my home.

A few months later, in New York, I returned to working on this book, which is about Birobidzhan, the concept of home, and knowing when to leave.

1

The man who made Birobidzhan famous had the gift of knowing when to run. That he lived into his late sixties is testament to his outstanding survival instincts. On his sixty-eighth birthday, he was shot to death, a final victim of the century's most productive executioner. He had been a writer who preferred to leave his stories ragged and open-ended, but his own life, which ended on what became known as the Night of the Murdered Poets, had a sinister rhyme and roundness to it.

David Bergelson was born on August 12, 1884, in the village of Okhrimovo, a Ukrainian shtetl so small there might be no record of it now if it were not for Bergelson's association with it. Three and a half years before his birth, Czar Alexander II was assassinated by a group of young revolutionaries that counted one Jew, a woman, among them. Five persons were hanged for the crime, but it was the Jews of Russia who bore the brunt of the national rage. After some years of acquiring greater rights and freedoms, as well as hope, the Jews found the law closing in on them, herding them back into the shtetlach. Pogroms swept through the Pale, brutalizing the enlightened modern Russian-speaking Jews along with their traditional parents.[1] Into this bleak, dangerous world came the surprise ninth child of an older couple.

The parents were rich and pious. Bergelson's father, a grain and timber merchant, spoke no Russian; he belonged to the last generation of Jews who could achieve wealth, success, and prominence entirely within the confines of the Yiddish-speaking world. His wife was younger and of a different sphere: a cultured woman, a reader. David Bergelson's education was an unsuccessful attempt to merge his parents' worlds. He was tutored by a *maskil*—a product of the Jewish enlightenment movement—who taught him to speak and write in Russian and Hebrew, in addition to his native Yiddish, but not, as the young Bergelson found out later, well enough to enable him to be admitted to an institution of higher learning. His father died when David was a little boy, his mother when he was fourteen, and David's wanderings commenced.[2] Losing one's anchors—and any sense of home—is essential for developing an instinct for knowing when it's time to run.

The teenager left the shtetl and stayed, by turns, with older siblings in the big cities of Kyiv, Warsaw, and Odessa, subsidizing their hospitality out of his share of the family inheritance.[3] He had a home, and a family, only so long as he could pay for them. This is another good lesson. One always has to pay to belong, and to have a roof over one's head.

One thing Bergelson seems to have always known about himself was that he was a writer. Any young writer must find his language, but rarely is the choice as literal—and as difficult—as it was for Jews writing in the Russian Empire in the late nineteenth and early twentieth centuries. In the cities between which Bergelson was moving, he was surrounded by Yiddish, Russian, Ukrainian, Polish, and Lithuanian speech. His command of these languages ranged from poor to limited. Then there was Hebrew, the language of his father's prayers and a new movement's dreams; as a teenager, Bergelson went through a period of fascination with the work of Nachman Syrkin, the founder of Labor Zionism. (Syrkin himself wrote in Hebrew, Yiddish, Russian, German, and English.) Bergelson tried writing in Hebrew and failed—it may be that his command of it was insufficient for writing, or it could be that the language, in his hands, did not lend itself to the modernism he was attempting. He switched to Russian, but this expansive language failed him, too, perhaps because he wanted to write stark, sparse prose and Russian demanded flowery vagueness. He finally found his voice in his long-dead father's living language, Yiddish.

A century later, when a crop of new academics rediscovered Bergelson, they would call his fictional characters "plastic," which is not only unfair but misleading. I have only an inkling, based on my own experience of being a stranger in a strange land, but I imagine that his characters are people as he saw them. The women were inscrutable, impulsive, unfair, inexplicably generous at times and unexpectedly cold at others. The men were lonely and displaced. They lived in their imaginations because they had no home and no interlocutor in the physical world. They waited for the future to happen, for a door to open and let them out into that world, but the world comprised only dead-end streets and circular roads that always led back to themselves and the ghosts they carried with them. His main characters invariably lived in a lone house outside of town, or spent their days in the woods, or walked around speaking to dead friends in their heads. When the plot suddenly broke the loneliness of one of his male characters, Bergelson's narrative focus would immediately shift away from him, to a darker, more desolate character. Could he not imagine companionship that can assuage loneliness? His second novel literally ended where the conversation between its male and female protagonists finally began.

No one wanted to publish that. The world of Yiddish fiction had grown lively and even crowded by the time Bergelson attempted to enter it, but it expected the very opposite of the young writer's desolate prose. Editors either rejected his work out of hand or sat on it for months, apparently at a loss. He had to insert himself into the Yiddish literary world personally in order to get things moving. He started making runs to Warsaw, the seat of the reigning kings of Yiddish literature. He showed up on editors' doorsteps to get their attention. He finally underwrote part of the cost of publishing his first book. The novel came out in 1909, when Bergelson was twenty-five, the result of five years not so much of writing as of striving to stake his place in the Jewish literary scene.[4]

When a man has no home but a great need of belonging, he must build his own world. This is the secret of the outcast, the émigré, the wandering Jew. Bergelson started shuttling between Warsaw, Wilna, and Kyiv, each city a focal point of Jewish culture. He became the center of the Kyiv

Group, which included the Yiddish-language writers Der Nister, Leyb Kvitko, and Dovid Hofshteyn.[5]

These writers' lives would intersect with Bergelson's for longer than would seem physically or historically possible. Der Nister was Bergelson's precise peer (they were in their twenties when they met); he had started out writing poetry in Hebrew but had never published a word of it. Then he switched from poetry to prose, from Hebrew to Yiddish, and from his given name to the pseudonym, which means "the Hidden One." His political sympathies ran to the Labor Zionists and the Territorialists, who believed that a land ought to be found for the Jews somewhere, not necessarily in the Levant but certainly away from the czars and their pogroms. Dovid Hofshteyn, five years younger than Bergelson, hailed from an unusual secular family: his father was a *maskil*, his mother a klezmer musician, his sister a Yiddish poet. Dovid himself began writing poetry as a child, in Hebrew, Russian, and Ukrainian, and brought all these languages to his membership in the Yiddish writers' brotherhood. Politically, he was a revolutionary. Leyb Kvitko was six years younger, which qualified him as Bergelson's protégé: he joined the Kyiv Group by correspondence from the Ukrainian city of Uman, where he published a handwritten journal in Yiddish, and later moved to the big city, to a big literary welcome in the small Yiddish-language circle.

These writers knew something about language that few others know. Even before my parents finally persuaded each other to leave the Soviet Union, I grew up hearing and reading a single lament. I knew beyond a shadow of a doubt that the biggest tragedy of emigration was the loss of language. Writers lost their readers, the story went, and they lost their ability to write: they lost their tongue. This was demonstrably not true. In fact, most writers my family knew and virtually all writers we read could not be officially published in the Soviet Union; my parents and uncounted other reader-distributors typed their work up on loud German-made manual typewriters, which produced a maximum of four carbon-paper copies, if the paper was thin and the stroke was heavy. Many of them, when they mustered the courage to leave the country or were forced out, found houses in the West that were willing to publish them in both Russian and other languages, found larger audiences, teaching gigs, and, in a few cases, even found fame. But my literary-critic mother and her friends and colleagues held to the gospel that one could write in one language and one language only, and that this language stayed alive only as long as the writer lived among people who spoke it. This meant that if we left the country, I could not become a writer.

I accepted this truth and, upon crossing the Soviet border, gave up all ambition of becoming a writer. I went to college to study architecture, dropped out, and backed into writing awkwardly and disbelievingly. The first language I was published in was English, but for decades I generally refused to read my writing in public because then I could hear my own accent. Later—much later, it seemed, after I had finally grown to believe that I was a writer—an entire generation of Russian Jewish émigrés writing in English came on the scene, as though they and their writing were the most logical things in the world. I found that I especially liked those of them who, like Anya Ulinich or Lara Vapnyar, not only spoke with an accent but also wrote with one.

It wasn't until long after that, not until I was working on this book, that I realized that Jewish writers had been making conscious choices about their writing language for more than a century. My mother had talked about language as though it were an immutable characteristic, a right or a burden bestowed at birth. I think she was speaking from both literature and experience. She had grown up behind the Iron Curtain, with poor—often laughably poor—language instruction, and it was only her extraordinary ability and perseverance that had enabled her to learn eight foreign languages well enough to read them but, certainly, never to write in them. Russian émigré writers whose works reached her lamented their lack of access to the living language, which affirmed her view of the lands beyond Soviet borders as some sort of a linguistic desert.

But the Jewish writers who grew up in the Russian Empire at the turn of the twentieth century were steeped in many living languages. Hebrew was the language of their studies and, for many of them, of their wildest dreams. Yiddish was the language of their homes and, more often than not, their streets. It also turned out to be the best language for describing what went on and what was said, sung, and felt in those streets. Russian was the language of higher education and secular discussion. A writer may have sought his language, and even found it, but more often he made a decision about the language depending on the topic, the context, and the audience. He might reshape a piece—or a book—originally rendered in Russian when rewriting it for an audience that would read it in Hebrew. Some readers would receive the piece twice, differently.

2

When Simon Dubnow, the greatest historian and theoretician of Eastern European Jewry, first wrote his *Letters on Old and New Judaism*, around the turn of the twentieth century, he used Russian. More than two decades later, he translated the essays into Hebrew, but he might also be said to have written them again in Hebrew: the times had changed, the country in which Dubnow lived had changed, and the language had changed, not coincidentally. In his lifetime, Dubnow lived in many cities, three or four or five countries, depending on who was counting and how, and wrote in three different languages.

It was Dubnow's concept of autonomism that, refracted repeatedly but not quite beyond recognition, became the idea behind the Jewish settlement in Birobidzhan. It was also his concept of a secular Judaism as the basis for national identity that, when I finally read it, in my forties, I recognized as the foundation of my own Jewishness.

Dubnow was born in 1860—a generation before Bergelson—in a shtetl in what is now Belarus. He moved to St. Petersburg in search of a secular education and lived there illegally for four years before giving up on getting into university in that city, then the imperial capital. He tried to study closer to home but finally returned to the shtetl, exhausted, emaciated, and humiliated: he had no income and could not physically survive away from his family. But soon he began writing on Jewish history and Jewish self-concept. At the age of thirty, he moved his family to Odessa, a center of Jewish intellectual and literary life at the time. His closest friends and daily interlocutors included Hayim Nahman Bialik, a poet who wrote in both Yiddish and Hebrew, and the essayist Ahad Ha-Am, who became his sparring partner in the public conversation about Jewish national identity and fate.

Dubnow and Ahad Ha-Am conducted their argument in Russian, through published essays they called letters. Dubnow considered the Jews to be a nation. (My Soviet documents specified that, regardless of my citizenship, my "nationality" was Jewish.) In fact, he wrote that the Jews were, from an evolutionary perspective, the most advanced of nations. They had no trappings of a nation—only the essence of one.

> When a people loses not only its political independence but also its land, when the storm of history uproots it and removes it far from its natural homeland and it becomes dispersed and scattered in alien lands, and in addition loses its unifying language; if, despite the fact that the external national bonds have been destroyed, such a nation still maintains itself for many years, creates an independent existence, reveals a stubborn determination to carry on its autonomous development—such a people has reached the highest stage of cultural-historical individuality and may be said to be indestructible, if only it cling forcefully to its national will. We have many examples in history of nations that have become dispersed among other nations. We find only one instance, however, of a people that has survived for thousands of years despite dispersion and loss of homeland. This unique people is the people of Israel.[1]

If Jewishness was a nationality, then one did not have to be religiously Jewish to remain a Jew. Converting to another religion, however, would be going a step too far because it would tear the person from the cultural fabric of his nation. "We aim only to negate the supremacy of religion, but not to eliminate it from the storehouse of national cultural treasures," wrote Dubnow. He called Jews a "cultural-historical" kind of nation, and he stressed that "the religion of Judaism is one of the integral foundations of national culture." Therefore, "a non-believing Jew may be counted as an adherent of Judaism so long as he does not identify himself with any other faith that conforms to his philosophical views."[2]

Part of what made the Jews what Dubnow called the "archetype of a nation" was the very lack of any trappings of a state, with its monopoly on and tendency toward violence. It was survival in diaspora that had shaped the Jews to near perfection.

> There is absolutely no doubt that Jewish nationalism in essence has nothing in common with any tendency toward violence. As a spiritual or historical-cultural nation, deprived of any possibility of aspiring to political triumphs, of seizing territory by force or of subjecting other nations to cultural domination (language, religion and education), it is concerned with only one thing: protecting its national individuality and safeguarding its autonomous development in all states everywhere in the Diaspora. It has no aggressive national aspirations even of the kind found among other peoples that lack political independence but live on their own soil and show the tendency to wipe out the national minorities living in their midst (for example the behavior of the Poles toward the Jews in Russian Poland, and toward the Ruthenians and Jews in Austria). The Jewish nationality is an outstanding example of a collective individuality which protects itself against attacks from the outside but never stops to attack on its own and is not able to do so. A nationality of this kind manifests the highest sense of social justice, which demands that the equality of all nations be recognized as an equal right of all to defend themselves and their internal autonomous life.[3]

It would follow that Dubnow disagreed with the Zionists. But his most urgent argument, early in the formulation of his view of Jewish identity, was with the assimilationists. He saw the real and immediate danger in the desire of so many European Jews to trade national difference for full citizenship. He called this tendency "national suicide."[4] Assuming that territorial and political sovereignty were off the table, Dubnow proposed that Jews fight for "social and cultural autonomy," which would include education in a Jewish language, community self-rule, and cooperation among Jewish communities living in the territories of different countries. In some of the European cities with significant Jewish populations, all of this was reality, or close to it, in the interwar period, but what Dubnow described as national rights often came at the expense of civil rights. The autonomist agenda called for securing national rights alongside full citizenship, as an essential part of it.

And then there were the Zionists. Early on, Dubnow had no patience for them. "Political Zionism is merely a renewed form of messianism that was transmitted from the enthusiastic minds of the religious kabbalists to the minds of the political communal leaders," he wrote. "In it the ecstasy bound up in the great idea of rebirth blurs the lines between reality and fantasy."[5] The Zionist idea of persuading the bulk of European Jewry to move to Palestine, of securing the right for them to do so, of then establishing a Jewish state there—none of this appeared the least bit realistic to Dubnow, and he saw the fantasy as siphoning much-needed energy from the business at hand, the task of securing Jewish autonomy in the diaspora. The Zionists argued that it was the autonomist idea that was, at base, a fantasy.

"The Jewish question exists wherever Jews live in perceptible numbers," wrote Theodor Herzl in his Zionist manifesto, *The Jewish State*. "Where it does not exist, it is carried by Jews in the course of their migrations. We naturally move to those places where we are not persecuted, and there our presence produces persecution. This is the case in every country, and will remain so, even in those highly civilized—for instance, France—until the Jewish question finds a solution on a political basis. The unfortunate Jews are now carrying the seeds of Anti-Semitism into England; they have already introduced it into America."[6]

In Dubnow's view, this Zionist argument was blind to the political and cultural shifts that had changed Europe in the nineteenth century, as well as to the opportunities they presented. Dreaming of Zion was bound to inspire the few to move to Palestine and the many simply to lose hope of seeing a future of equality, either in their current homeland or in the ancestral one. Over the decades, noticing that many more Jews were finding their way to Palestine than he had expected, he moderated his critique of political Zionism, though he still could not envision a Jewish state. More important, he stressed the simple mathematics of the problem: even if hundreds of thousands moved to Palestine, even if a million did, the majority of the world's Jews would still be living in dispersion. Before the Second World War, more than nine million Jews were living in Europe, most of them in lands that were or had been part of the Russian Empire.

In Odessa, Dubnow chaired the Committee on Nationalization, a discussion club that included writers of his acquaintance and other thinkers, like Meir Dizengoff, who would later become mayor of Tel Aviv. On April 7, 1903, the committee hosted a large audience that gathered to listen to the young writer Vladimir Jabotinsky, who had recently pronounced himself to be a Zionist. On that day, Jewish refugees began streaming into Odessa from Kishinev, a city just over a hundred miles to the north, in Bessarabia. Jabotinsky had grown up there.[7]

The pogrom in Kishinev had begun a day earlier, on the last day of Passover. It raged for forty-eight hours. At the end, forty-nine Jews were dead and some five hundred had been injured or raped. This was not just the first pogrom of the new century; it was the first pogrom that had been openly, and pointedly, incited by the regime.

Dubnow did what writers do. He called the essay "A Historic Moment (The Question of Emigration)." It was the ninth of his "letters" on Jewish identity. He noted, "The last twenty years bequeathed to us two forms of national self-help: (1) energetic work in the lands of the Diaspora; (2) mass exodus from the place of danger." The story of Jewish emigration from Russia had begun with the pogroms and expulsions of the early 1880s and, wrote Dubnow,

a mighty historic revolution has been taking place before our eyes: the transfer of the chief center of our people. Just as four hundred years ago the center of the Jewish people was transferred from western to eastern Europe and Jewish national hegemony passed from Spain to Poland, and then to Russia, so part of our great center is now being transferred by an uninterrupted exodus from Russia to other countries. Where is the main stream of migrants going? Not to our ancient homeland, Palestine, where, in spite of all our efforts, we succeeded in bringing only 20,000 persons during the last two decades (if the urban population is added to the agricultural); not to Argentina, where only several hundred families were settled on the land at the cost of millions of dollars, but to North America, especially to the United States. Close to a million Jews left Russia during the last twenty years and nine-tenths of this number went to North America.[8]

Dubnow called the wave of emigration he had been witnessing "second in importance only to the expulsion of the Jews from Spain in 1492." By his estimate, between twenty-five and thirty-five thousand Jews a year had been leaving, mostly for North America. He expected the Kishinev pogrom to prompt another hundred thousand to leave. Editing the essay for publication in Hebrew years later, he noted that he had underestimated by about half.

As for the first option for national action—"energetic work in the lands of the Diaspora"—it was Jabotinsky who founded a Jewish self-defense movement in Odessa then. He also threw himself earnestly into the study of Hebrew and changed his name to Ze'ev. Dubnow joined the self-defense effort and a larger campaign to educate the public. It drained him of the time and energy required for writing and ultimately drove him to leave Odessa, though not to emigrate from the Russian Empire.

In 1905 Dubnow moved to St. Petersburg, where the first Russian revolution was about to usher a parliament into existence. The second and third revolutions came a dozen years later, shattering the world Dubnow inhabited. The events of 1917 devastated him—unlike many Jewish intellectuals, he seemed to have no illusion that a Bolshevik Russia would be good for him, or for the Jews. He left for Berlin in 1922. His eldest child, a daughter, was living in newly independent Poland with her family; a son and a daughter and their families stayed behind in Moscow.

What I find remarkable about Dubnow's perception of Berlin is how quickly the worry set in. Emigration necessarily involves a charmed honeymoon, which serves as a payoff, however illusory, for the deprivations and the sheer misery of waiting to leave one place for another. In Dubnow's case, there were months and years of not knowing whether he would be able to leave Bolshevik Russia, then protracted and stressful negotiations regarding his library, and then, finally, complicated, difficult, fragmented travel to Berlin itself. Yet within a year of arriving, he wrote in a letter, "We are suffering now together with Germany, and Germany itself may make us suffer still."[9]

Still, Berlin was the new center of Jewish intellectual and literary life. Writers and thinkers from the Russian Empire had fled there, and young and old now frequented the same cafés and competed for the same commissions from American Jewish publications—getting paid in dollars was the best way to survive Germany's galloping inflation. Dubnow managed, and in 1930 he and his wife were even able to buy an apartment. For the first time since emigrating, the writer had his desk as he wanted it and his books around him. But on the eve of Yom Kippur in 1931, the secular thinker wrote to a friend, "I have returned to my work, but my mood befits the Day of Judgment: I sense that a black cloud is hovering over the world."[10] His instincts were still in good working order.

An exodus from Berlin began, tentatively at first, and then, following the March 1933 election in which Adolf Hitler's Nazi Party triumphed, everyone Dubnow knew seemed to be leaving. (Altogether, about 130,000—roughly one in five German Jews—emigrated in the 1930s, some 50,000 of them to Palestine.)[11] For a person who has emigrated once, the option of changing countries is always on the table—and the suitcase, packed, is always standing by the door. Some people returned to Soviet Russia; some sought refuge nearby, too close: in Austria and Czechoslovakia. Some schemed, successfully, to secure a visa to move to Palestine. A significant number were relocating to Paris, which seemed, for the moment, to be housing Eastern European Jewry's endlessly movable intellectual center.

Dubnow knew that he had to leave, but he struggled to choose his destination. Paris seemed to him too noisy and crowded. He considered Zurich but ultimately settled on Latvia, the tiny Baltic state that had only recently become an independent country. "Many things speak in favor of Riga," he wrote to a friend. "The environment will feel more familiar. We will be closer to our children, both those who live in Warsaw and those who are in the Soviet Union. We are leading a sorrowful life here, quiet on the surface but full of internal anxieties. The period of transition is difficult, the émigré's state of mind a burden. My friends in Palestine are surprised at my decision not to move there: they cannot understand that at our age the change of climate, language, and the entire way of life would take our remaining energies, which we need for other things."[12]

Dubnow had picked Latvia in part because the government's policies promoted what he had long advocated: Jewish self-governance. The tiny country had a network of Yiddish-language schools, several Jewish newspapers, and even a permanent Jewish theater. But by 1934 its politicians began emulating neighboring Germany—or, more likely, seeing in German politics the inspiration and an excuse to promote ideas that had been bubbling under the surface. In 1934 the prime minister disbanded the parliament, establishing authoritarian rule. Overnight all civic organizations, including Jewish ones, ceased to exist. The slogan "Latvia for the Latvians" rapidly gained currency; it referred to ethnic Latvians and excluded Jews. Still, there were no explicitly anti-Semitic laws, and Latvia even accepted several thousand Jewish refugees from Germany.

Dubnow began to consider moving to Poland, even though by this time that country also had an authoritarian government, one that had instituted some blatantly anti-Semitic policies. He was playing a key role in YIVO, the Institute for Jewish Research, formed in Wilna (the Polish name for Vilnius) in 1925. In addition, his older daughter, Sofia, was living in Warsaw with her husband, Henryk Erlich, one of the leaders of the Bund, a party that promoted the Jewish labor movement. But then, one day in the summer of 1935, Dubnow and his daughter and her family boarded a small riverboat in Poland. Their boat, as it turned out, was already carrying a large group of Polish college students from the city of Poznan, near the border with Germany, who had been visiting some Catholic monasteries in the east of the country. The students grew livid at being joined on board by Jews. They declared their intention to throw Erlich overboard (apparently, they were willing to spare the lives, if not the dignity, of Dubnow, who was by now an old man, and his daughter and her small children). The captain docked the boat at the first opportunity and begged the Jews to leave. Dubnow retired the idea of emigrating to Poland.[13]

"My life can now be measured in the quarter-centuries," Dubnow wrote in 1935. "It is a great gift to a historian, to have lived in three generations, three dimensions, as it were, for this allows him to better understand the mystery of the change of epochs. But it can be a great sorrow, too, if the transition leads to the worse, for then the fear arises that one's life might end during a dark period. We are living through a frightening time, and only my double faith in my lives as a Jew and as a chronicler gives me the strength to withstand it all."[14] Here was a life goal articulated: to die in a better time and place than the ones into which you were born.

That goal seemed more and more elusive. "It has become just so hard to breathe in Europe today," Dubnow wrote in a letter to a friend living in Paris in January 1938. "It is too hard to fight the degradation of entire nations."[15]

At the end of that year, following Kristallnacht—the Night of Broken Glass—and the concomitant deportation of thousands of Jews from the Third Reich to Poland, Dubnow wrote, "For the first time in all of the centuries of modern history have we witnessed a pogrom carried out by a government, but this also, for the first time, drew protest from all over the world."[16]

Would protest and sympathy translate into actual help? Dubnow wrote passionately about the need to organize the mass emigration—evacuation, really—of Jews from Europe, but at the end of a letter detailing this need, he took himself out of the picture: "I am not at all concerned about the need to save myself from the storm. I am not contaminated by the panic raging around me—and anyway, where would I run? I must hope that the small Baltic states will remain neutral."[17] He decided that he was safe in Latvia.

It had been more than thirty years—moved by the Kishinev pogrom of 1903—since Dubnow had begun focusing on the need for Jews to have the option of leaving any land where they were in danger. Addressing critics of fleeing as a solution, he wrote, "If you deprive the Jew of the hope of changing his place, the hope that he will be able to escape from danger, if things are bad, to a country where thousands of his brethren have found refuge, you will crush his soul into the dust. Then he will really despair because he will feel hemmed in on all sides and deserted by the whole world without refuge from oppression and persecution. What you say is quite true, the Jews stand with one foot in Russia and with the other in America; but if they were to stand with both feet on the Russian volcano, they would not have a firm foothold for fear of the possible terrors of the near future. . . . If those who pin all their hopes on the liberation movement now bury the emigration movement, they will be forced to exhume it later."[18]

Dubnow envisioned a multipolar Jewish world, with centers in the United States, perhaps Argentina and South Africa, certainly Poland and Palestine. He despaired when he considered Russia after the Bolshevik revolution, though more than a million Jews still lived there. He grieved the destruction of the Jewish civilization in Poland at the start of the Second World War, but he did not live to see the world in which the restoration of that center was inconceivable. When he died, he could still imagine a worldwide web of Jewish communities that had secured the autonomy sufficient to maintain Jewish languages and cultures and the communication necessary to help one another and to provide escape routes if a community was endangered. Unlike the Zionist fantasy, this vision was rooted in reason. Unlike the catastrophe to come, it could be imagined.

3

Bergelson came of age in a Jewish cultural world framed by the arguments of Dubnow and his contemporaries. He found himself in Odessa in 1916. Dubnow had left the city a decade earlier, but his friend Bialik was still there, in body if not in spirit—his heart was already in Palestine. Still, Bergelson and Bialik became fast friends, and Bialik was part of Bergelson's wedding party. "Tsipeleh," Bialik said, addressing the bride in his speech, "don't give him to the Bolsheviks."[1] This was either the end of 1917 or the beginning of 1918;[2] the Bolsheviks had already overturned the democratic provisional government and instituted what they called the "dictatorship of the proletariat," but Jews in Odessa could still joke about them.

Bergelson was getting married at the relatively old age of thirty-two. The bride's name betrayed the fact that her parents did not speak Russian; in that language Tsipe Kutsenogaya means "lame chick." In fact she was young, blue-eyed, and anything but lame: she was strong enough to see the writer through the second half of his life.

Then the pogroms started. Not that they had ever stopped. Still, the Jews had not seen brutality on this scale in nearly four centuries. During the civil war of 1918–22, the different entities that called themselves the White Army, each led by its own general, attacked the Jews for their perceived support of the Bolsheviks and disloyalty to the czar. The self-proclaimed Ukrainian national army, commanded by Symon Petlyura, attacked the Jews for being Jews. The anarchists, led by Nestor Makhno, engaged in random violence, as did a long list of what were essentially roaming gangs. In all, more than two thousand pogroms were carried out in the three years following the Bolshevik revolution, killing nearly two hundred thousand Jews and leaving half a million homeless.[3]

Bergelson had lost his vigilance at the wrong time. His young wife was pregnant. He decided to leave Odessa and contrived to take Tsipe out of the city, to her home shtetl, Gaisin, outside of Vinnitsa. He himself then went to Kyiv, promising to return before the baby came. The promise must have rung fantastical, if not false, from the beginning: in a land where new borders appeared and old ones shifted every day, separations had a way of becoming permanent.

Yiddish life in wartime Kyiv was more active than ever. In January 1918 Ukraine had passed a law allowing minorities to form autonomous governments with broad rights, including taxation. For the next two years, even as Ukraine kept changing hands, an effort at developing a Jewish national autonomy continued. Within this effort, Bergelson took on editorial posts one after another, running short-lived and occasionally imaginary journals and fleeting cultural organizations. Bergelson's son, Lev, was born in August, the month of his own birth, in Gaisin, during a pogrom. Traveling there was out of the question: a Jew journeying by rail could not expect to live.

Bergelson arranged for a Ukrainian peasant named Petro to go to Gaisin, buy a horse and cart, load Tsipe and the three-month-old baby into it, and travel the endless 150 miles to Kyiv. Tsipe was under strict instructions not to speak whenever someone who fancied himself king of the road stopped the cart to check its contents; her blond hair and blue eyes allowed her to be passed off as Petro's wife only as long as she did not utter a single heavily accented word in Ukrainian. It was a good thing the baby had not yet acquired language.

Decades later, asked to write an article about his father, Lev began with a lament: "When I think back to my earliest childhood . . . I can . . . hear the snorting of horses, the creaking of carts, the rattle of train wheels, and whistles of locomotives. . . . These pictures of the distant past settled in layers on later events in my long life, which I also see now as a long string of migrations from one city to another, from one country to another, associated each time with separating myself from a familiar environment, from friends and relatives, and, finally, from my beloved father."[4]

"A long string of migrations" is the Jew's legacy. What Lev didn't remember was that the first major move of his life placed him by his father's side, and his father was living through one of the happiest times of his life. He was at the center of things, a sort of minister of Jewish affairs, running the Kultur-Lige, a cultural empire that was, it seemed, the epitome of Dubnow's autonomist vision, or at least its cultural part. The founding declaration of the Kultur-Lige linked Yiddish culture to democracy and proclaimed it a "forward-looking" culture. It was democratic because it spoke the language of the masses, and it was the culture of the future because it was secular.[5]

In addition to Bergelson's old partners from the Kyiv Group, the Kultur-Lige included another writer who would travel on parallel paths with Bergelson for the rest of the two men's lives. Perets Markish had come to Kyiv soon after he finished his service in the imperial army. He was now a prolific poet; Hofshteyn and Kvitko lauded his writing, though it left Bergelson pointedly cold. Still, the Kultur-Lige took into its fold not only every agent of Yiddish cultural production Bergelson could identify but also, at least nominally, dozens of schools, libraries, theaters, and universities.[6] Moments of pure joy fed by great ambition would, however, give way to despair. Wave after wave of Jewish refugees from the pogroms swept into the city. No number of magazines and plays could feed them or shelter them. In fact, Bergelson and his overactive circle could not be sure of feeding or sheltering themselves for much longer. In 1920, the Bolsheviks took final control of Ukraine. By May of that year, though the work continued, the activists of the Kultur-Lige were spending their time talking about ways to escape. Bergelson wrote a letter addressed to "all friends of Yiddish art and culture in America." He sent it to friends he had lost to that continent and to others, persons he had never seen.

Amidst shockingly inhuman conditions, among ruined towns and villages razed, drowned in blood, and now obliterated, in the small desolate island of Kiev lives a small exhausted group—a group of Jewish writers, sculptors, painters and poets who, in great anguish and pain, drag out what is left of their lives over here. . . . Will you provide this exhausted group of artists with visas and the material resources to travel across to America?[7]

They waited for a response through the summer; none came. There must have been days of calm and even joy, when chestnut trees bloomed all over Bergelson's beloved Kyiv, when the nights were warm and food seemed, if not plentiful, then at least within reach, in a land that was bursting with fruit and grain. Autumn brought fear of the impending cold and the hunger they knew the winter would bring. Tsipe fell ill with typhoid fever. Almost as soon as she recovered, a group of writers with Bergelson at its center crowded into a cattle car outfitted with a wood-burning stove and traveled north to Moscow. The five-hundred-mile journey through the freezing winter took ten days.[8]

The Bolshevik government in Moscow was just then in the process of putting its Jewish house in order, screening out the Zionists and the Hebraists for their predominantly anti-Bolshevik stand and pulling the Yiddishists into the fold. Bialik and about a dozen other prominent Hebrew writers left the country, narrowly escaping death or jail.[9] Dubnow, while not a Zionist, was a historian and a philosopher, and thus doubly inconvenient; he left. Markish moved to Warsaw. But Bergelson, for the first time in his life, seized his position on the side that had the power: he was a secular Yiddishist who believed in the organizing power of the word. He was granted housing, in an apartment repossessed from a bourgeois family, who most likely continued to occupy one or two rooms in the flat. The Bergelson family's territory was a single room, grand, empty, and unheated.[10] His new job title was Yiddish editor for the Yevsektsia (the name was short for "Jewish Section"), the Jewish committee of the Communist Party. He tried to start another literary magazine.[11]

The Bolsheviks' internationalist rhetoric, the job title, the rare privilege of a whole room notwithstanding, Bergelson's instincts told him that this time he should keep moving. A poet friend working at the Lithuanian embassy fixed him up with a Lithuanian passport and, less than a year after arriving, the Bergelsons left Moscow. He stationed his family in a small village outside of Kovno, the new Lithuanian capital, since Wilna was now a part of Poland. He then set off on a reconnaissance trip to Berlin—no easy task, since the way to Berlin lay through Poland, with which Lithuania had severed diplomatic ties. He had to travel by sea; once again it took him many days to traverse a short distance. In Berlin, he found a lively Yiddish literary scene—and a publisher, who was ready with an advance.[12] Bergelson returned to Lithuania to collect his wife and child and undertook another arduous journey by boat; all three were terribly seasick. "Seriously and firmly we settled in Berlin, and spent thirteen happy years there," his son would write decades later. "Yet, it seems to me, we always regarded ourselves as temporary and not particularly welcome residents."[13] Bergelson had been living in other people's houses and other people's cities for more than twenty years; he had learned that home was always elsewhere.

But Berlin was the center of the universe. Its literary market was growing almost as fast, and as obscenely, as the German mark was falling. Several publishing houses specialized in Jewish literature. After the Great War, Berliners seemed hungry to read anything and everything, and the publishers counted on even greater demand than they had a right to. They figured, for example, that a vast readers' market awaited them in Russia, where the Bolsheviks had fairly well annihilated book publishing, and they reprinted Russian and Jewish-Russian classics in Russian and other languages.[14] After five years of running for his life, Bergelson suddenly discovered that he had become a classic writer: a Berlin publisher put out a six-volume edition of his collected works.[15]

Everyone was coming to Berlin. Bialik was already there, as was his friend Dubnow. Der Nister and Kvitko, members of the Kyiv Group, came. The American Jewish Joint Distribution Committee, a relief organization, supported the poorer immigrants with grants.[16] Anyone who did not have American dollars was poor, growing hundreds of times poorer every day: marks were counted by the hundreds, then by the millions, then billions, until, finally, a loaf of bread cost a trillion German marks. In addition, everyone was homeless in Berlin; refugees from Germany's own war and from the Russian Revolution swelled the number of city residents so much that the local authorities instituted an apartment-rationing system. A rental contract required official permission, which was granted with difficulty and revoked with ease.[17]

The Bergelsons moved from one small, unheated, and unsecure Berlin apartment to another for a couple of years, until they finally managed to settle in a garden house located on the property of Tsipe's wealthier relatives.[18] Bergelson returned to a comfortable routine familiar from long-ago days of relative peace and stability. He wrote in solitude in the mornings, behind a desk littered with pages and adorned with an overflowing ashtray and a chocolate bar, from which he took his reward when he deemed a page well written. He played the violin to relax, favoring lyrical melodies in a minor key. In the afternoons, he entertained artistic friends. Some of them were passing through on their way from somewhere to someplace, in the great Jewish resettlement of the interbellum; some belonged to the groups of young aspiring Jewish literary types who made the rounds of all the great men who now lived in Berlin.[19] In the evenings, Bergelson often held court at the smoke-filled Romanisches Café, where every émigré faction—the Zionists, the Bundists, the Yiddishists—had its own marble table. He listened to other people's poetry, played chess, which he had recently grown to love, and made his argument.[20]

His cause, as ever, was modern Yiddish literature, a schizophrenic construction that might have existed fully in his imagination only, for this was the sole place where the austerity of modernist writing grew naturally out of the chaos of shtetl life. His opponents were Markish and an old rival of his from Kyiv, Moyshe Litvakov, who was now a leader of the Yevsektsia in Moscow; both argued for a Yiddish literature divorced from the past, a literature for which Yiddish was only a language, whatever that would mean. Here was something Dubnow, who saw in Yiddish the promise of continuity between shtetl life and city culture, between the past and the future, had not foreseen: an effort to keep the language while deleting the tradition and history behind it. Bergelson minced no words when writing about this Soviet stance: "Jewish communists in Russia decide that there are no longer Jews in the world," he wrote in the American daily *Forverts* in March 1923. He accused Soviet Jews of "scratching off their own Jewishness until blood starts to run."[21]

Starting in December 1924, Bergelson presided over his own Jewish émigré cafe, the Sholem Aleichem Club, opened with the help of some friends and Aaron Singalovsky, the leader of Rehabilitation Through Training, a Jewish educational movement. Housed in a converted apartment, the café drew crowds with its acclaimed Ashkenazi kitchen, evening lectures, and concerts, including, it was said, one where Bergelson and Albert Einstein got out their violins and played together.[22]

Meanwhile, Bergelson's fellow refugees were growing wary of Berlin. German cabinets kept failing, resigning almost as soon as they took office, while the economy went from bad to ridiculous. "I am free, I am working; daily I receive page proofs from various publishers. Am I happy?" Dubnow wrote in his personal journal on the first anniversary of his arrival in Berlin. "No. It is impossible to be calm while breathing the air of anxiety. I am observing the ruins of Europe crumble ever more, burying the ideals and dreams of a recent past . . . extinguishing any hope for a European peace. As seductive as the promise of calm was in the spring of 1922, it has dissolved by the spring of 1923."[23] Half a year later, Dubnow made this entry: "It has come to this. Berlin is rehearsing a street pogrom, complete with the beatings of Jews. Yesterday the price of a loaf of bread went up from 25 to 140 billion. Crowds started attacking bread stores while in the Jewish neighborhoods they beat up Jewish passersby. Germany is facing a crisis: it is going to drown along with all of its culture, either in a sea of *black* or in a sea of *red*."[24] The most remarkable part of this diary entry is the date: autumn 1923, a full ten years before the "sea of black" officially arrived in Berlin.

In 1924, Bialik moved to Tel Aviv, taking his publishing house, Dvir, with him. Der Nister and Kvitko edged in the opposite direction, relocating to Hamburg for now, to work for the Soviet trade mission. Markish moved to Moscow in 1926. Bergelson stayed put for the moment—as did Dubnow—perhaps because both enjoyed the constant affirmation of local publishers, who were reprinting their earlier work, and the influx of cash from America in the form of commissions for articles.

Writing for the wealthy New York Yiddish daily *Forverts* was the best assignment going in Berlin. With its circulation of two hundred thousand,[25] it could afford its editor Ab Cahan's fascination with the Berlin Yiddish scene. Cahan kept a full-time bureau chief in the city, an Odessa-born economist, and regularly scouted out writers to adorn his literature page. An offer from Cahan promised salvation. "For the first time in my life, I have been seduced by the offer of money," wrote Dubnow, whom Cahan had approached in January 1923. "The promise is of a minimum of 25 dollars per article, which, at today's exchange rate, is a million German marks. This could actually save me from the apartment terror: I could purchase part of a villa or start making million-mark payments to landlords, which would keep their ire down and I could do my own scholarly work then, for it is impossible to work atop a volcano."[26] Soon enough, he did buy an apartment of his own, set up his library as he wanted it, and settled in to work.

Bergelson's anxiety, on the other hand, rose along with his expectations. He pestered Cahan with long letters, complaining that the American held pieces too long and paid too little. "All of this would be acceptable if the times were different," he wrote in May 1924. "I would simply ask myself: what do you want from Ab Cahan? Ab Cahan must consider the interests of his paper first. If he publishes me only once, or at best, twice a month, it is a sign that the paper doesn't need me three or four times a month. But I could only think this way if my family and I were not experiencing hunger. It is very different when one finds oneself in the loathsome, inhuman situation of permanent hunger. One then begins to become upset. One begins to think: even if I were only a small cog in a piece of machinery, I would still deserve to be fed. If *Forverts* needs me only on special occasions, then I should be valued no less than a typesetter, no less than a . . . bookkeeper [or] a janitor who cleans *Forverts*'s offices." Bergelson might have exaggerated the depth of his despair, but he conveyed the level of his fear.[7]

His belligerence paid off: he got a regular salary. Starting in August 1925, the weekly pay was a respectable forty dollars. But the writer's relationship with Cahan never found its footing. Conventional wisdom in Yiddish-writing circles held that Cahan did not need Bergelson at his paper; he needed his name. Cahan claimed, privately, to be a fan of Bergelson's writing, but in publishing practice he was hypercritical and conservative. He held the short stories for weeks and months on end. He used Bergelson more as a journalist than as a writer of belles lettres, which meant the spotlight was Cahan's, not Bergelson's.

If one had to sum up Cahan's complicated political views, one might say he was a prescient anti-Communist socialist. He had published John Reed's *Ten Days That Shook the World*—but, oddly for a Yiddish-language publisher, he parted ways with the Soviets on the subject of assimilation: he preached Americanization just when the idea of Jewish autonomy had great traction with the Bolsheviks. Early on, Bergelson wrote virulently anti-Bolshevik pieces for *Forverts*, attacking the Yevsektsia with the sort of deadly precision characteristic of one who had known and perhaps loved the men he was attacking. Cahan never acknowledged the importance of Bergelson's contribution to the debate, and Bergelson grew to resent him and, eventually, to regret his own stories. He could not afford to align himself so completely with someone who refused responsibility for his survival.

On February 5, 1926, Bergelson submitted to *Forverts* a story called "An Unusual Ending,"[28] the tale of a young writer struggling and failing to portray a revolution that draws him in but evades understanding. The tone of the story left the reader wondering whether it was the protagonist, the author, or the reader being mocked.

Less than a month later, the Moscow Yiddish-language daily *Der emes*

(The truth), the official paper of the Yevsektsia, now edited by Litvakov, printed Bergelson's letter of repentance. "I confess," he wrote, "to having erred in 1923 by openly coming out in print against the Yevsektsia. . . . I think the question of my returning to Soviet Russia is inopportune under present circumstances [because of hostility engendered by my attacks]. . . . I find that the exile that I suffer here is a deserved punishment for my earlier failure to understand the difficult position of the Yevsektsia."[29] Bergelson was hedging his bets, positioning himself as one doing penance in exile, one who might someday ask to be taken back—if one were desperate enough. His flight instinct was still in good working order.

4

Rumors flew. Yiddish speakers in Berlin whispered that Bergelson was plotting a return to Moscow, where he might try to become a timber merchant, like his father, or conjure up some other sort of lucrative enterprise.[1] It was hard to tell which was more absurd: the idea of the writer becoming an entrepreneur or the idea of anyone doing so in Soviet Russia. In fact, Dubnow was arguing that the end of private enterprise spelled the end of the autonomists' hopes for Russia. Speaking at a major Jewish political congress in Zurich in August 1927, Dubnow laid out his vision of the battle for Jewish rights. Revolutions often presented opportunities for the Jews, he said. The French Revolution had granted the Jews civil rights while robbing them of their cultural rights. The Russian revolutionary period of 1905 through 1917 had prompted the Jews to formulate the agenda of full citizenship that would include cultural autonomy. The Bolshevik revolution, however, had ended constructive work for cultural autonomy in Russia, said Dubnow, and now he saw hope only in the Jewish communities in Poland, the Baltic states, and the Balkan ones—for Jewish activists in those countries had recourse to the League of Nations, which could act as guarantor of the Jews' rights within their states.

The Soviet Union took umbrage at Dubnow's assessment of Jews' rights in the Bolshevik state. A highly placed party bureaucrat gave a talk a few months later, a rebuke to Dubnow; he pointed out that Jews in Soviet Russia had more rights than anywhere else and, unlike Jews in Poland and Lithuania, were not confronted with anti-Semitism. Both claims were highly contestable, but in his response, written in April 1928, Dubnow chose to focus on a deeper issue. Granting full civil rights to the Jews, he wrote, would not compensate them for the losses they had suffered from losing the right to be traders and merchants after the Bolsheviks eliminated all private enterprise. If most Jews living in the Russian Empire had been poor, now they were destitute. Physical poverty devalued any rights they had on paper.

Was Bergelson, who was well off by Berlin standards, really considering plunging into the economic disaster zone that was Russia? The absurdity of the proposition was surely behind the rumors that he stood to make a fortune in timber. Cahan, the *Forverts* publisher, was among those who struggled to make sense of Bergelson's *Der emes* article. As soon as he saw the story, in March 1926, he telegraphed his Berlin bureau chief: "What are the real facts about B and his letter for Soviet Russia—please write at once."[2] Whatever response he received, Cahan in short order formed his own theory explaining his writer's behavior.

"I got to know Bergelson fairly well in Berlin," he wrote to his bureau chief. "I felt that he was making plans to return to Russia. . . . I also noticed that certain stories of his were heading in the same direction—laying a foundation for 'subjugation' to the Bolsheviks. I brought this to his attention and explained that we couldn't print such stories. Even a few of the stories that we *were* able to print were of the same sort. After his letter appeared in *Emes*, I received letters from several comrades in Europe, who expressed the opinion that after writing such a letter, he should no longer have a position at *Forverts*. I responded that I preferred to take a philosophical attitude toward the situation, and that if he were to write things that we could print, we would do so. . . . But many of his stories and other pieces in our possession remained unpublished, all for the same reason: they are not literature, but propaganda."[3]

For Bergelson's part, he staged his break with his publisher the way one of his female characters might take her leave from a lover: with sudden and calculated cruelty. On May 1—International Workers' Day—he resigned from his position at *Forverts* with a cool letter to Cahan, citing delays in the publication of his pieces and asking for any unpublished manuscripts to be returned.[4] In fact, he had already taken up with other publications. He had spent months trying to recruit Yiddish-language writers to his newest periodical venture, *In shpan* (In Harness), a literary journal of pro-Communist writing. In the inaugural issue, published in early 1926, he had written that Warsaw and New York no longer promised a future for Yiddish writers. He dismissed New York Jews as willing to relinquish their Jewishness in order to blend in with Americans, and Jewish life in Warsaw, he wrote, had been seized by the Orthodox and the Zionists.[5]

While Dubnow gradually mellowed toward the Zionists, Bergelson grew increasingly intolerant of them. The way the Zionists handled the ideas of home and language fed Bergelson's resentment. He missed his home, and he had little patience for people who fantasized a home they had never seen. But it was their cavalier attitude toward language that pained him the most: the Zionists had no use for Yiddish, the language of Bergelson's stories and arguments. It was early—one might say premature—to perceive in 1926 that Yiddish could become an endangered language. But even though New York City had five Yiddish-language daily newspapers, Bergelson, who had never been there, saw New York Jews switching to English. In Eastern Europe, the Zionists' Hebrew-literacy campaigns were rapidly displacing Yiddish-language education. That left Soviet Russia, where there were no Zionists—legally, at least—and no Americans.

At the end of May 1926, Bergelson published his first story in *Freiheit*, the youngest of New York's Yiddish dailies and the only one that unequivocally supported the Soviets. In a note appended to the story, he informed the readers (and perhaps Cahan and most certainly whoever was monitoring the Yiddish media from Moscow), "I find it necessary [to state] that I have severed my ties with the American newspaper *Forverts* and no longer publish my work there."[6] This first story painted a heroic and optimistic picture of "Jewish life in Russia in a few years," under the watchful guidance of the Yevsektsia and the Soviet Jewish intelligentsia. *Der emes* in Moscow printed this piece simultaneously with *Freiheit*.

In August, Cahan published a retort to Bergelson's *In shpan* piece. "I know that he doesn't believe one word of his article," he asserted.[7] He may have been right, but when the article came out, Bergelson was in the Soviet Union, for the first time in five years, partaking in a bizarre ritual designed to prove his commitment to the Bolshevik cause.

5

B ergelson had gone on assignment for *Freiheit*. He spent a week in
Moscow, filing lovely happy dispatches on life in the Soviet Union.
He then traveled to the Crimea, where he reported on Jewish territorial
settlements, set up by the Soviets and funded by American Jewish communities. The stories were long on red banners and grand pronounce-
ments and short on the detail that had once marked Bergelson as a great
writer. Nothing in the pieces communicated the sense, smell, or sound of
a real place—it was as though Bergelson had been writing with his eyes
and ears shut. But this was how propaganda pieces were done. The author
reserved his passion for ideological traitors—the Zionists who were using
the Crimea as a way station to Palestine, the shtetlach refugees who hoped
to re-create a middle-class life on a collective farm. Bergelson, who would
return to his charming garden house in Berlin and his marble table at the
Romanisches Café, had no mercy for these pettily bourgeois Jews.[1]

Before returning to Berlin in late September, he stopped in Moscow
for what amounted to a public flogging, a ritual reserved for returning
émigrés. A meeting was called, with Litvakov, his old friend and nemesis,
presiding. Bergelson came wearing patent leather shoes—a shining mark
of Western decadence—as though asking for the ridicule he immediately
got. Litvakov reproached him for the "emptiness" of his earlier writing—
this after Bergelson had just spent a month filing some of the emptiest
prose produced in this emptiest of times. To thundering applause, he
mounted the stage to acknowledge that, while he had been prepared for
the criticism, it had exceeded his "worst expectations." Then, playing his

part in this sadomasochistic play, he read a story called "The Red Army Soldier." The audience of writer-comrades took turns trashing the story. Then all those present professed satisfaction with the ritual. "All and all, I love this evening," said Bergelson, addressing the people who had just spent hours humiliating him. "This evening, with its strictness, binds me to you even more tightly than before."[2]

Then he returned to Berlin, flummoxing the rumormongers. He was not rushing to go back to live in Russia. It was as though he knew it was inevitable. For now, all he observed in Berlin were storm clouds, ominous rather than dangerous, but he understood that they would not simply dissipate. Perhaps what made his new writing so terrible was that the requisite passion in it was manufactured out of a sense of hopelessness. Bergelson was like Mirl, the female protagonist of his best novel, *When All Is Said and Done*, who agrees to marry a man she does not love and awaits her wedding date in dull despair, finding relief only in the vain hope that the engagement can be called off (it will not be) or the marriage will not be consummated (it will be). After the wedding, she is by turns impassive and impulsive, looking for a love that will take her away from the prison of her marriage, finding many takers and no feeling in her heart for any of them.

Like Mirl, Bergelson revisited those who had once jilted him. He traveled to New York, arriving as a third-class passenger on December 1, 1928, and was greeted on the shore by a group of Yiddish literati. He turned theatrically back toward the water, gestured to the Statue of Liberty, and exclaimed, "Your lie is displayed naked before the whole world." Less than a decade earlier, Bergelson had been tired and poor and begging to be helped, and had been ignored. Now America was just as oblivious to the plight of European Jews, who sensed, with varying degrees of acuity, that they were in danger in Kovno and Warsaw, in Berlin and Paris. Russia might be demanding that Bergelson beg for forgiveness, but America had already shown itself to be as indifferent to begging as it was to all other things. A week after landing, Bergelson spoke at the Central Opera House to a crowd of thousands, some drawn by the scandal that had surrounded his departure from *Forverts*, some brought in by their habit of attending all Yiddish literary events, and some bussed in as part of a field trip for the association of natives of Okhrimovo, the shtetl where he was born.[3] This American attention was mistimed and perhaps misplaced, for America—and its community of Jewish writers in particular—was the lover whose rejection had forced Bergelson into the arms of the husband who now humiliated him.

Like Mirl, Bergelson made emotional, dangerous statements and seemed to have no recollection of them a day later. Or perhaps he was engaging in the cacophonous play of all propaganda, sending out as many messages as possible and listening carefully for any response to inform his further action. In an interview for *Der tog*, a Yiddish daily higher in tone and more moderate in politics than *Forverts*, he lashed out against Soviet anti-Semitism and had some choice words for the "déclassé Jews" of the Soviet Union. Then he granted a counterinterview to his own paper, *Freiheit*, in which he claimed that *Der tog* had misrepresented his views. Individual writers offered to help him make his home in New York. But there were no job offers or legal papers attached to these offers, and Bergelson bristled, said no, and went on at great length about his dislike for the Jewish community in America.[4]

Occasionally, he tried to explain. The Jews in America, he said, thought Jewishness was religion with a bit of Zionism mixed in. But Jewishness was culture, and culture was language, and their five Yiddish dailies were not long for this world because the language was fading, dissolving into the great American abyss of false security. Bergelson could always sense when something was about to die. Just as he knew that he could never make the American Jews understand.

On the way back to Berlin, Bergelson stopped off in Warsaw for two weeks. He had spent time in this city as a boy, and he had visited it again as a young writer, seeking the blessing of his elders. Here the smell of impending death was even stronger. He complained that the air in the city "stank."[5]

Weeks after Bergelson returned to Berlin, a wave of riots in Palestine left 133 Jews dead, hundreds more wounded, and the rest terrified. "A hundred and fifty thousand Jews living atop a volcano" became a catch-phrase.[6] The Yiddish press in America invoked the rhetoric of pogroms, and the American Jewish community mobilized to support a new defensive ethos among the Jews of Palestine. The Palestinian Communist Party joined in this mobilization but was quickly reprimanded by the Communist International, which sided with the Arab members of the party;[7] with more than a hundred Arabs killed in the riots, the disturbances could hardly be compared with the pogroms in Russia or Ukraine, where armed gangs massacred a defenseless population. *Freiheit* was the only one of the Yiddish dailies to follow the Comintern line; this cost it a number of its readers, writers, and funders, but Bergelson remained, even if the paper now had trouble paying regularly as agreed.[8] Ever since Bergelson had left his lucrative gig at *Forverts*, Tsipe had been working as a typist at the Soviet trade mission, supporting the family.[9] Working at the Soviet trade mission was another common rite of passage among those who wanted to return to Russia.

Bergelson had burned all his bridges, made the rounds of all his old suitors and told them off, and now he led a ghostly existence in Berlin, hoping perhaps that his engagement to Moscow would prove a long one. He still held court at the Romanisches Café, but so rarely that one of the regulars dubbed him its *balmusef*—the cantor who officiates at special services only.[10] He took another trip to the Soviet Union in 1931, saw friends and former rivals who warned him that returning to Russia would be difficult—as if he did not know, as if he had a choice—and he came back to Berlin and publicly announced his intention to repatriate.[11] This may have been an effort to keep himself convinced, and it was certainly a part of paying his dues: he had to continue earning the right of return. His trips were growing longer and more frequent, but still he kept Tsipe and Lev in the garden house in Berlin and one foot in the Romanisches Café.

6

Soon after coming to power, the Bolshevik government adopted a strategy of trying to harness nationalism to preserve the empire rather than pull it apart—by granting each self-identified ethnic group a form of autonomy, ranging from a national village soviet at the bottom to a national republic at the top. Between nationalization and some warped idea of justice, Jewish autonomy became bound to agriculture; the Jews, who had not been allowed to own land in czarist Russia, would now toil at collective farms. Aided financially by American Jewish communities, dozens of such settlements appeared in the Crimea and southern Ukraine in the first decade of Soviet rule, generating enormous resentment among besieged local peasants. A top Ukrainian party official warned the Politburo in a letter in 1926, "Innumerable attempts to create exceptionally favorable conditions for Jewish agricultural settlement, to the detriment of the interests of the broad mass of Soviet agriculturists, has called forth from the latter a sharply heightened anti-Jewish mood."[1] At the same time, as the Soviet regime eliminated private enterprise large and small, increasing numbers of Jews lost their livelihoods. A study conducted on the territory that used to be the Pale of Settlement confirmed that "the living conditions of the broad Jewish masses have not only failed to improve but have, in certain ways, become worse." Between 30 and 40 percent of Jews in Ukraine, Belarus, and western Russia had no source of income.[2]

The government continued to insist that the Jews must now live off the land. In 1926, Mikhail Kalinin, the titular head of the Soviet state, sounded an ominous note in his address to a conference of the Committee for the Settlement of Toiling Jews on the Land (OZET):

> The Jewish population faces a major challenge—the preservation of its nationality. To accomplish this, a significant portion of the population has to be converted to a compactly settled agricultural population of at least several hundred thousand. Only if these conditions are met can the Jewish masses have any hope for the continued existence of their nation.[3]

What he apparently had in mind was an underpopulated region on the border of contested Manchuria. The following year, a group of agronomists spent the summer in the region, defined by the rivers Bira and Bidzhan, studying the settlers' prospects. They produced an eighty-page report that reads like a litany of the difficulties the Jewish settlers would face. In fact, it reads like a list of arguments against the very idea.[4]

First there was the terrain: mountains that were, while not especially tall, prohibitively steep and plagued with rock formations that met at such sharp angles that they could not be traversed even on horseback. The valley was largely swampland.

Then there was the weather. Winters, which began in October and lasted through April, were harsh; summers brought torrential downpours interspersed with days of scorching hot weather.

And then there was the evil that warranted the report's most eloquent paragraph:

> We should especially like to underscore the significance of the blood-sucking insects—the exceeding quantities of gadflies, mosquitoes, and midges, which, over the course of the two summer months, cause extreme suffering to cattle and man. The bloodsucking insects affect farming by lowering the animals' productivity over the summer and by creating insurmountable obstacles to conducting work involving horses in the light of day. To fight the bloodsucking insects, the locals use smoke and strong-smelling ointments applied

to cattle. People wear netting and head gear but, generally speaking, grow accustomed to the evil that are the insects.

And, finally, there were the locals. Most of them were Cossacks sent there by a decree of the czar in the 1860s to help fortify the border. They arrived decades before the railroad stretched this far, and they endured unspeakable hardships before they managed to tame the land enough to live on it. The area was also home to a small population of Korean-Russians, clear second-class citizens compared to the Cossacks (among other things, czarist decrees granted the Korean families only half as much land as the Cossack ones). To complicate things further, marauding gangs of ethnic Chinese known as the *honghutzu*—literally, the red-bearded ones—terrorized the locals, especially the Koreans, who cultivated opium poppies, the local currency of choice.

The report closed with five pages of conclusions, mostly warnings that the Jewish settlement project would be forbiddingly difficult. Getting people there would be hard: there was the railroad, but the supporting infrastructure was in disrepair. Getting cattle to the people would be harder still—and more expensive. Housing construction would have to happen fast—the weather afforded no more than a couple of months' opening, provided the settlers arrived in June—but building would be difficult, since much of the region had already been deforested by man and fire. This was also one of the reasons the local Cossacks tended toward a nomadic lifestyle: firewood was scarce. The agricultural project, in other words, looked unrealistic, and the experts, agronomists all, made the polite suggestion that the settlers consider going the industrial route. A full year of intense preparations, including the construction of roads, residential buildings, and melioration systems, was necessary before any settlers could arrive. No settlers should plan on coming before 1929—and no more than a thousand families in the first year and a couple thousand families each year after that.

The report also mentioned that the local population felt anxious about the planned Jewish invasion.

The Soviet government ignored virtually all of the committee's recommendations and decided to settle the region immediately, aiming to move a million people to the area within ten years.

The name Birobidzhan, after the rivers Bira and Bidzhan, would come later. For now, there was a dilapidated train station called Tikhonkaya, "Little Quiet One," which was someone's polite way of saying "godforsaken." The first trainload of settlers arrived in April 1928; within a few weeks, 504 families and 150 individual settlers had arrived, roughly doubling the population of Tikhonkaya, which at that point boasted 237 houses, a single elementary school, and one shop. There was nothing else: no post office, no telephone service, no paved roads, and no sidewalks but for some wooden planks floating in the mud.

Two strains of settlers arrived. On one side, there was a steady trickle of Jews relocating from abroad, mostly Yiddish speakers who had fled the Russian Empire in the early twentieth century and were now returning from Argentina, the United States, and even Palestine. These people were no strangers to hardship, but they had generally lived in places with existing infrastructure: running water, electricity, schools. The stream coming from the other side were the poor and desperate from the decimated shtetlach of Ukraine and western Belarus. They had known misfortune and danger, including pogroms that had run as long as most of them could remember, but faced with the prospect of living in tents indefinitely, most of them—roughly two-thirds—turned back. It snowed that May. It is safe to assume that most of those who stayed either had no home at all to go back to or no way of scraping together the cash for a return ticket (90 percent of the cost of inbound tickets for those coming from the Soviet Union had been covered by the settlement program).[5,6]

A number of those who stayed were directed to eight plots of land about thirty miles southwest of Tikhonkaya, where in the summer of 1928 they founded Birofeld, the first Jewish collective farm in the Far East. The farm subsumed a tiny Cossack village called Alexandrovka, marking probably the first instance in history when a Jewish name supplanted a Russian one. Over the following year and a half, three more collective farms appeared: Amurzet (so named for the river Amur and OZET, the Jewish land-resettlement body); Valdheym ("Forest Home" in Yiddish); and IKOR, named for the U.S.-based organization that was the chief sponsor of both the farm and its inhabitants—the settlers who had arrived from abroad. IKOR was to be a collection of communes jointly administered by Soviet and American Jewish authorities, in accordance with a utopian plan tolerated by the Soviet authorities because it drew U.S. backing. In 1929, an IKOR delegation visited the commune and gave its seal of approval to immigration to Birobidzhan from outside the Soviet Union.[7]

In the summer of 1928 there were torrential rains, causing flooding that washed out what little the new settlers had managed to plant, stymied by the late arrival of seeds. Their cattle arrived late, too, and were felled by an anthrax epidemic that raged that first year. The settlers at Birofeld, though they managed to put up eighteen houses over the summer, faced a cold winter of relentless hunger, surrounded by their ruined fields and foreboding woods, where tigers and bears roamed. Most of these collective-farm pioneers from the shtetlach were men who had traveled ahead of their wives, planning to send for them once they were settled; now they wintered in isolation, the nearest people dozens of miles away, unreachable in the absence of cars or even horses that would be strong enough to make the journey. Jews who had not been assigned land immediately upon arrival actually fared better: local Cossack families took some of them in, keeping them warm and fed through the long winter—and teaching them to fish, among other things.[8]

Out of hundreds of settlers, only a handful had ever worked on a farm—and that had been in the agricultural south of the Russian Empire, where the climate was kind and the land was accommodating. Few of the new arrivals knew how to clear a field, how to choose horses or cows, or how to care for them. They set about building clay-walled huts—traditional Ukrainian dwellings that could not keep out the extreme cold or stand up to the local rains. Many of the settlers—the furriers, the cobblers, the tailors—had brought the tools of their old trades with them and wanted nothing more than to start skinning, cobbling, and sewing again. After the first miserable winter on the collective farms, they fled—some back to Ukraine, some only as far away as Tikhonkaya, which they now viewed as a city, and where they hoped they might be able to work again.

Inexperienced new settlers immediately materialized to take the place of those who had escaped. "Often it would happen in the middle of the night, when everyone was asleep, that a new crop of settlers would suddenly appear in Valdheym," recalled Leyba Shkolnik, one of the founders of that collective farm, in an interview recorded in 1935. "And they never asked whether Valdheym needed new settlers and what kinds of jobs they could be used for. They just sent them in, with their wives and children, and they all needed to be fed. And this was still at a time when there was no [workable] land in Valdheym, when we were still just clearing it. The authorities who assigned new arrivals to their place of settlement were not good to the people. The usual thing to do would be to bring them in during a heavy rain. They would drive them in, drop them off in the middle of the night in the rain, and leave."[9]

Four years after the first settlers arrived, in the summer of 1932, the area was again hit by uncommonly heavy rains that led to flooding, destroying all of the settlers' accomplishments. "Almost all of our crops were under water," recalled Shkolnik. "Even in the few greenhouses that were not flooded, everything we had been growing was killed. . . . And then things got worse. We had no straw. Cows started dying off. What grass we had managed to salvage wasn't enough to feed even two hundred cows. It got worse than it had ever been. People started running. They ran during the day and they ran at night. The ones who had saved a little something over the years ran under the cover of night so they would not have to share what they had with the collective farm. Before winter came, almost half the people had abandoned Valdheym."[10]

7

In the fall of 1932, Bergelson undertook the longest journey of his life. He traveled the Trans-Siberian Railway all the way through Siberia and beyond, disembarking just fifty miles shy of the border with China, in the budding Jewish autonomy of Birobidzhan. The Jews of Birobidzhan welcomed him grandly, as if he were a long-lost descendant of a royal Yiddish tribe. A plenary session of the settlement council convened in his honor. He toured the new collective farms in the company of local authorities. He participated, as a guest of honor, in the celebration of the fifteenth anniversary of the October Revolution—an unprecedented role for a foreign national.

The price had been named. In exchange for a dignified return to Soviet Russia, Bergelson would sing the praises of Birobidzhan. He got to work at once.

All around chains of mountains rose up, high and rounded, their summits mantled in peaceful blue clouds, as though this was the way it had always been, for thousands of years. All three distant horizons were filled with these mountains. Their dawn was a crystal of pure light, shimmering in every hue. The sun offered powerful heat and an expansive glow. In the blue, marvelously lofty skies there was no trace of a cloud. Oceans of light caught at the pale blue smoke on the distant horizon and scattered it. Peeking out through the diffusing pale blue smoke were the blue summits of the mountains, myriad rivers gleaming in the sun, valleys narrow and wide, expanses of taiga and mixed fields, and all of this taken together was the land that the authorities had allocated for the working Jews, all of this together bore the name:—Birobidzhan.

He returned to Berlin in mid-December 1932. He postponed all meetings and assignments to get on with the Birobidzhan book.[1] The urgency could not be underestimated. On January 30, 1933, Adolf Hitler was named chancellor of Germany.

Bergelson's biographers note that fifteen-year-old Lev was harassed in the street.[2] But this was certainly not what distinguished Bergelson from the hundreds of thousands of Jews who remained in Germany after January 1933. What made him different was his instinct for survival and action. He sent his wife and son to Copenhagen, because he could. He wrapped up in Berlin and joined his family in Denmark briefly. In Copenhagen in March, he wrote a letter to a friend, detailing his desire to press on with a book on Birobidzhan, at the expense of his fiction writing: "This socialist construction, which is part of the general socialist construction in the Soviet Union and therefore has the same great scale and great future, the completely new and extremely interesting human material, with these people's enthusiastic and heroic way of overcoming difficulties, the rapid development of a new multifaceted life on a multifaceted basis—everything was so unexpected and overwhelming for me that, as happens when one is destined to witness an event of great importance, I was simply unable immediately to start portraying the grandeur of what I could see all around me."[3] He took another quick trip to Paris, where so many of the former-Russian, formerly of Berlin Jews were now hoping for the best; then he returned to Copenhagen, collected his family, and moved to Moscow.

Family lore has it that when Tsipe took a look around the vast, empty Moscow train station, she exclaimed, "We have perished."[4] This may, of course, be true, as even family lore sometimes is, but given Bergelson's options and his history, what choice was there? Berlin, with its streets patrolled by Hitler-Jugend? Palestine, where a hundred and fifty thousand madmen insisted on living atop a volcano (and where the British had instituted visa quotas following unrest)? New York, with is vapid Jewish culture and its utter lack of job prospects, where Bergelson would have every chance of joining the ranks of paupers? Soviet Russia had two million Jews, many of whom could read Bergelson's books, being readied for reissue by Soviet publishing houses, or see his plays, which had been staged by the state Jewish theater—and this, in turn, made Bergelson unexpectedly flush. Royalties, paid in inconvertible rubles, had been accumulating in Moscow for years.[5] The rumormongers may have been right, after all, about the lure of wealth that had called Bergelson to Moscow. Perhaps it was a win-win proposition: Bergelson would get to make a living as a writer while aiding Moscow's plan for solving the Jewish question—and if the question had to be posed, then the solution proposed by Moscow seemed preferable to all the others.

8

What did he really see in Birobidzhan when he first visited? The cold would already have set in; the mud with which the wooden sidewalks did a losing battle in the warmer months would have been frozen. A family legend had Bergelson walking the muddy streets all night, returning to the hotel in the morning "ashen-faced and covered in mud," so shocked and dismayed was he at what he had seen.[1] Like so many family legends, this one probably expresses the needs and knowledge of others. There would have been no mud. The days would have been short, light, and crisp. The sky would have been wide and the sun stubborn, making for prolonged periods of dusk, which Bergelson, a child of the relative south, might never have experienced before. His description of Birobidzhan—its "three distant horizons," its "pure" and "shimmering" light, the powerful sun, "marvelously lofty skies," "myriad rivers gleaming in the sun," two variations on the word *expanse* and five uses of *blue* in a single paragraph—show that he was genuinely awed, after a decade and a half spent running from one crowded city to another in an overstuffed train car, or as a third-class ship passenger, to be offered something so plainly huge: "and all of this taken together was the land that the authorities had allocated for the working Jews, all of this together bore the name: Birobidzhan."

Tikhonkaya had been so renamed by the Central Committee of the Communist Party just a year earlier; what had been a village was now termed an "urban workers' settlement."[2] Twelve long two-story barracks-type buildings had been constructed, more or less doubling the amount of residential space in the city. The barracks had no running water; each family was allotted a single room along a long corridor, which was crowded with belongings that did not fit in the rooms, where every square inch did double and triple duty. The publisher of the weekly *American Hebrew and Jewish Tribune*, David Brown, visited Birobidzhan at the same time as Bergelson and reported, "I have learned that the impossible is possible. I saw barracks that housed several families at the same time. Some of them had no windows but had no lack of ventilation: the wood for their construction had not been properly dried out and as it settled now, cracks formed, freely letting in the cold October air."[3] These living conditions, though, would for several more decades remain fairly typical for all Soviet cities, overcrowded now as a result of massive rural flight. All over the country, people were running from their villages as the Soviet regime requisitioned private property, imposing collective farming and, more often than not, policies that led to hunger, sometimes policies that produced mass famine. Here in Birobidzhan, the reasons for abandoning collective farms were the same as anywhere else in the country: the overwhelming fear of a long cold and hungry winter.

The year Bergelson came to visit, the year of the second great flood, about 40 percent of the new settlers had turned back—the highest proportion in three years. Altogether, between nine and ten thousand of the Jews who had arrived starting in 1928 remained in Birobidzhan.[4] Most of them seemed to believe that the agricultural experiment had failed. A new industrial plan was taking shape. An IKOR delegation that visited the region in 1929 had recommended that Birobidzhan settlers focus on building factories large and small, and it had promised to help. Various industrial equipment had been arriving in regular shipments from America, and now, following the flood of 1932, the local party authorities had finally drafted a five-year plan that projected that nearly three-quarters of the population would be working in industry. Or so they told David Brown, who was a former banker and one of the leading American fundraisers for Birobidzhan.

"They tried to impress me by demonstrating the factories that are already functioning in Birobidzhan," reported Brown.

The friendly thing to do might be to leave them without comment. . . . The factories manufacture, as they like to say here, twenty-seven kinds of products: bricks, limestone, carts, cart parts, soap, shoe cream, turpentine, firewood, baskets, rattan furniture, chairs, desks, wardrobes, suitcases, shoes, clothes, etc. . . . The factories are cooperative ventures, initial funding for which was provided by the government, while most of the equipment was provided by IKOR, the American organization. . . . The factories are located either in old buildings or in poorly constructed new ones. In most cases, these buildings also serve as the residences for the workers, a regrettable situation as each family has use of only a single barracks-style room with no running water or other conveniences. . . . The quality of the workmanship here is poor, primitive for lack of proper equipment and high-quality raw materials as well as insufficient worker expertise and a poor organization of labor. There are other reasons, too: poor oversight, lack of discipline, a lack of desire to excel, since everything will be bought anyway—not a single product has been returned to date. Additionally, the working conditions are poor to say the least, and have a negative impact on these people's health. After visiting several factories, I came to the conclusion that this kind of industrial production is a result of poor planning: it was begun solely to create work for settlers who had despaired of working in agriculture in Birobidzhan. If I said that they shouldn't have started production at all, I would be going too far, but continuing production on such a weak foundation would yield regrettable results. It is a matter of time—a short time, I believe—before Russians start demanding quality goods and the factories of Birobidzhan, such as is their condition now, will be unable to compete.[5]

Bergelson was part of the same tour Brown was taken on. In fact, I suspect that a recurrent character who first appeared in his fiction after this trip to Birobidzhan was based on Brown.

The wind lifted a cloud of fine snow over the roofs and spread it again. It shed some light over the long street, with its deep frozen footprints in the iced-over mud. They looked as though left by giant boots that walked on their own, without the aid of feet.

The door opened. In walked a tall, light-haired man wearing a fur, unbuttoned, on top of an overcoat. A crooked half-smile rested on his pale face; he introduced himself self-consciously, as though the need to state his name embarrassed him. He slowly removed his eyeglasses, wiped them off with a suede cloth, and slowly replaced them, fixing the earpieces carefully and closing his eyes to ensure that the glasses assumed their proper place. It might have looked as though the eyeglasses had been placed upon his face by someone else and he merely, magnanimously, allowed this to happen. He made a chewing motion with his thin, slightly crooked lips, and said as he approached the desk,

"I am Prus, the economist. I have been to see you before."

He sat down as slowly as he had done everything else and extended his hand, which held several sheets of paper covered in his handwriting.

"This is the plan I am taking to Moscow," he said, scanning the walls and the ceiling with his eyes. "In New York I am well known as a specialist in matters of colonization. I spent some time at the IKOR collective farm, where American settlers live. . . . I state my position openly."

Increasingly, he sounded as though he had been insulted.

"This is what I think. The tiny pieces of land they are trying to work here, amid the swamp, are worthless. It's ridiculous! Even America leaves vast lands empty and imports bread from Canada. Alaska, for all its riches, spent a long time living without its own food production. I have said it before and I will say it again: the collective farmers should be shifted to the construction of a furniture plant. Just give me a chance to build a factory or two on the Amur and I will export their production and in return flood the area with bread from Manchuria. I want to explain this to you. . . ."

He was feeling hot. His eyes scanned the room ever more quickly, searching for a place to put his fur coat. He was beginning to take off his coat when he noticed a hand holding his sheets of paper, extended toward him, and heard the response:

"Take this. You can keep it. We have nothing to discuss."[6]

The story is set in November 1932, when Bergelson and Brown were both touring Birobidzhan. Brown was the hapless American, well-intentioned and potentially useful to Birobidzhan, with his weekly paper and his access to wealthy and equally well-intentioned American Jews, but apparently deaf to the music of Birobidzhan. Bergelson was the one who heard it: it was the music of Yiddish.

There were six Yiddish-language schools in Birobidzhan. There was a Yiddish-language newspaper, *Birobidzhaner shtern* (Birobidzhan Star), edited by an old acquaintance, the writer Henekh Kazakevich. There was a printing plant under construction; until then, the newspaper was typeset and printed in one of the barracks, often by the light of oil lamps or even candles.[7] There was even book production: a volume of poems called *Birobidzhanstroy* (The building of Birobidzhan) was printed in October 1932, launching the local publishing enterprise. The book had sixty-two pages, a press run of three thousand, and an eighteen-year-old author,[8] who, to Bergelson, may have been the single most important argument in favor of Birobidzhan.

Emmanuil Kazakevich had founded a Yiddish writing group in the Ukrainian city of Kharkiv, where his father, Henekh, was a prominent literary figure. The younger Kazakevich called his group Bird's Milk, an allusion to a saying (of ancient Greek origin, recycled occasionally in Russian) referring to extreme wealth. At the age of seventeen, Kazakevich became obsessed with Birobidzhan and not only moved there but persuaded most of his fellow Bird's Milk members to join him. "That's the place where we'll really be able to spread our wings," he promised.[9] His parents followed him to Birobidzhan a year later.[10]

Kazakevich was something of a new and improved version of Bergel-son. The older writer, the literary organizer of the Pale, had been self-conscious, hypercritical of his own writing, which had a cloistered and highly regimented form. As the literary soul of the new Jewish quasi-state, Kazakevich was overconfident, hyperenergetic, and impulsive. He had wholeheartedly adopted this expansive land; at the time of Bergel-son's first visit, in fact, the teenage poet was employed as the head of the Valdheym collective farm. He also functioned as a one-man hospitality committee, at least whenever new writers arrived in Birobidzhan. He would greet some of them at the resettlement headquarters with offerings of bread and butter, honey, and local salmon roe, which seemed all the more fantastically generous following a ten-day train journey.[11] He would take others on long nighttime walks through the crisp snow, stopping in the spotlight provided by the moon to declaim his own poems and his translations of Heine, Shakespeare, and Lermontov.[12]

In Bergelson's case, he proposed a hike to the scenic hills about fifteen miles from the town in the direction of Birofeld. Bergelson was nearing fifty, and his small frame had started to grow heavy. He had to acknowl-edge that he would not make it. "I'll have to get a car," said Kazakevich, stating the obvious and the obviously impossible, and disappeared. He returned a short while later, aboard a truck—one of only about ten in the entire region. Bergelson and Kazakevich and two more poets—a young man who had followed Kazakevich from Kharkiv and a young woman who had come, incredibly, from Poland by way of Palestine—piled onto the bed of the truck and began the rough journey over an unpaved road. Presently, Kazakevich began to sing. The popular Soviet tunes sounded familiar to Bergelson, even though he had spent most of the last decade abroad: all had been written by Jewish composers, and all had easily rec-ognizable klezmer origins. The songs had titles like "Moscow in May" and "My Country Is So Broad." Kazakevich sang in Yiddish, which sur-prised his young companions.

"You like?" he asked. "I just translated them today. Seems to work."

Kazakevich proceeded to give the group a detailed walking tour of the hills, lecturing them on the vegetation. "Here is a poplar tree," he would say. "It grows very fast, so we'll be planting it along city streets and in the parks."

On the way back to town, Kazakevich recited his own poem—later to become an epic—called "Citizen Taiga Has the Floor."[13]

Bergelson might have suspected that this was the only place in the world where young people, plural, were writing poetry in Yiddish. He placed himself in the service of Birobidzhan. On January 4, 1935, the Warsaw-based paper *Der fraynd* printed his manifesto.

WHY I AM IN FAVOR OF BIROBIDZHAN

1. All activity on behalf of Birobidzhan, which is part of the great Soviet Union, is activity on behalf of the socialist enterprise in its entirety.

2. Birobidzhan is one of the most important and prominent fronts in the establishment of a classless society.

3. The desire to become a "mirror" of what is being accomplished in Birobidzhan, with every plot of earth, every new house, and every manufacturing plant becoming an "open book" where I plan to expend all my working hours.

4. Birobidzhan, which is an undeveloped region on the border of "the imperialist world," gives one the pleasure of creating history, in the fullest sense of the word.

5. As a Jew, I feel more intensely in Birobidzhan, the only autonomous Jewish region and a future Soviet republic, the purpose of the national Soviet policy, under which all of the Soviet Union's national cultures will develop under equal conditions.

6. In Birobidzhan I will help build a glorious Jewish culture, socialist in form and national in content, which can serve propaganda purposes as well as a concrete model for the liberation of nations in the Soviet Union and for other nations in capitalist countries.

7. Refusing to work in and on behalf of Birobidzhan would be

both against my own personal interest and against the interests of our entire Soviet collective.

8. I want to work in and on behalf of Birobidzhan, because I wish to partake of those fascinating, delectable juices of life that our Soviet regime bestows upon me.[14]

Reason number 7 breaks my heart. He was a cornered animal. Was he unable to hide it? Was he still hoping that someone—Lady Liberty, perhaps?—would hear him this time? But then what? By the time this manifesto was published, Bergelson had been in Moscow a few months. Upon their arrival in that city, Tsipe may or may not have pronounced, "We have perished,"[15] but the move had changed everything. No longer was Bergelson the wandering Jew: once one came to the Soviet Union, one could not leave. (This was true until the 1970s, when a new generation of Jews secured the right to emigrate—and Bergelson's only granddaughter became one of the first Soviet Jews to move to Israel.) He had voluntarily surrendered his freedom to travel in exchange for the protection of a state that offered him a home. That Tsipe's dismay was immediate is eminently believable: the family had traveled by rail through Belarus, had seen hordes of the living dead, hundreds and thousands of people in the end stages of starvation who had gathered in the railroad stations, looking for a way to escape the nightmare.[16] Then they had arrived in Moscow, and after a dozen years spent in interwar Berlin, a city of excess and extremes if ever there was one, the stark and pervasive poverty of Soviet life could only have been a shock.

But even before the move—indeed, in order to earn the right to move—Bergelson had postponed all other tasks to create his first work of socialist realism, an undertaking unthinkable just a few years ago. The main character in *Birobidzhaner*, published in 1934, is an American misfit who cannot find his place in the Soviet Jewish socialist workers' paradise because he is motivated by money while everyone else is driven by ideals.

By Soviet standards, the Bergelsons were living extraordinarily well. Useless anywhere else, Bergelson's Soviet money was enough to finance a large apartment in the center of Moscow; a special dispensation allowed him to own property. Markish reported in a letter to the Yiddish novelist Joseph Opatoshu in New York: "Bergelson lives like a count! He has never in his life had a more prosperous time—both creatively and financially. An apartment is being built for him. And until it is completed, the government is paying a hotel 100 rubles a month for him and he is growing as broad as he is tall from the proud pleasure of it!"[1]

In 1935, Bergelson celebrated his fifty-first birthday in Moscow and left for Birobidzhan. He was on assignment for a Yiddish-language anthology called *Two Five-Year Plans*, to be published in 1937. Greeted and treated like royalty again, he went everywhere with first party secretary Matvei Khavkin and party executive committee chairman Joseph Liberberg. Bergelson had formed a surprisingly strong bond with Khavkin, an ill-educated and rather crude man who had accepted that Bergelson was the "Jewish Maxim Gorky," as he had been told when they were first introduced. For Bergelson's part, he spared no effort greasing the wheels. He described Khavkin as "a deeply and exceptionally devoted comrade, a likable fellow, a former tailor, a Bolshevik who grew up to become a person of eminence. I am entranced by his genius, his talents, his marvelous energy, and the tremendous idealism that this man of the people carries with him." Liberberg, a Yiddish scholar from Kyiv whom Bergelson had actually known in his past life, elicited no such praise.

The three men appeared together at a gala reception for a "special migrants'" train from Kyiv on October 12. This was a terrible time to alight in Birobidzhan, at the beginning of the long winter, which promised nothing but cold and privation for new arrivals, but he seemed too caught up in the unceasing celebration of Birobidzhan to take note of this. The following day, at a reception in honor of the new arrivals, Bergelson announced that he would be making his home in Birobidzhan. He received a standing ovation. Two weeks later, *Birobidzhaner shtern* published what was in essence another manifesto, this time intended for consumption within the Soviet Union. Here were the arguments:

1. The transformation of Birobidzhan into a Jewish autonomous region despite numerous difficulties.
2. The achievements of the previous year that had surpassed anything that could be imagined from a distance.
3. Only here could a Jewish Soviet writer work effectively.
4. The hope that this decision would accelerate the process of turning the district into a republic.
5. The opportunity to do interesting and effective work alongside Comrade Khavkin.
6. The desire to bring about a revolution in the minds of the Jewish intelligentsia so that they would start to move to the autonomous region.[2]

The announcement may have been part of a negotiated deal: Bergelson might never have had any intention of actually living in Birobidzhan, but making a show of it would inspire settlers to continue to come from America, Poland, Germany, Lithuania, and all other places where Jews read the Yiddish-language press.[3] But it was also in keeping with Bergelson's custom of maintaining a destination in reserve, one foot constantly out the door. The mechanisms of Soviet terror worked in unpredictable ways, often dependent on the fervor or fear of the local authorities, so maintaining two residences in the country was wise. In a nation that had largely succeeded in eliminating private property, Bergelson was slated to become the owner of multiple homes: in January 1936, the Birobidzhan authorities passed an act "setting aside land for the construction of a one-story house for the writer D. Bergelson as well as the construction of a center for writers," with an eye to those who would be following his example and moving to the region in large numbers.[4]

What was happening in Birobidzhan had often been, and would often be, repeated in the Soviet Union: after people were placed in conditions demonstrably unsuitable for living, after thousands fled and died, in a few years life seemed to settle into some semblance of stability. Once again, the Soviet experiment had demonstrated through great human sacrifice that people can survive anywhere. More than eight thousand people arrived in 1935, and none gave up—a remarkable reversal following a year in which more than half the newcomers turned around and left.[5] That year, the Jewish population of Birobidzhan would have roughly doubled.[6]

It was in May 1934 that the Central Committee of the Communist Party of the USSR granted Birobidzhan the status of the Jewish Autonomous Region, a major step toward achieving the coveted status of a national republic, the apogee of Soviet-style autonomism. At the end of that year, the local authorities inaugurated their institutions of power;[7] a complete set of councils of workers' deputies, courts, and representatives in the federal Nationalities Council went along with the new status.[8] In August 1936, the Central Committee of the Communist Party of the USSR declared the Jewish Autonomous Region to be a Soviet Jewish culture center, in which "masses of working Jewish people will develop their own state-structure,"[9] thereby affirming the region's ambitions and promising lavish funding for cultural institutions. "For the first time in the history of the Jewish people, its burning desire for a homeland, for the achievement of its own national statehood, has been fulfilled," the resolution declared.[10]

By this time, the young Kazakevich had left his job as chairman of a collective farm and was directing the construction of a theater. This would be the first in a series of stone buildings that reflected a grand aesthetic plan for Birobidzhan laid out by Hannes Meyer, a Swiss-born

architect who had been one of the leading lights of Bauhaus before falling
out with Walter Gropius and moving his team to Moscow to build socialism. The plan called for a large modernist city on the left bank of the Bira
River, but all that materialized were a few beautiful constructions on the
right bank, including the theater and the regional hospital, completed at
roughly the same time. Before the theater building was finished, an entire
troupe had arrived, trained by the great Solomon Mikhoels in Moscow
and dispatched to work in Birobidzhan[11] at the request of twenty-year-old
Kazakevich, who had traveled to the Soviet capital to recruit actors for
the theater.[12]

In February 1936, all of Birobidzhan rejoiced to receive a visit from
Lazar Kaganovich, secretary of the Central Committee, commissar of
communications, one of Stalin's closest allies, and certainly the most powerful and most prominent Jew in the Soviet Union. His was anything but
a cursory visit. He gave a two-hour talk to a meeting of party activists.
He attended a gala production of Sholem Aleichem's comedy *Di Goldgreber*
(The gold diggers) at the theater and declared that "the time has come
to bring to the stage the heroic moments in the history of the Jewish
people."[13] He had dinner at the Khavkins' house and praised their traditional Jewish cooking,[14] the importance of which he stressed in some of
his Birobidzhan speeches. He also suggested that Birobidzhan should host
a large scholarly conference on the Yiddish language.[15]

Inspired, the cultural and party elites of Birobidzhan got to work.
The actors and the local authorities met to rename Kazakevich's theater
the Kaganovich State Jewish Theater. Bergelson and Liberberg set their
mutual antipathies aside to organize the Yiddish conference, which would
bring together language and culture scholars from all over the country to
discuss issues of dialect, orthography, grammar, and newspaper and literary language. The conference was scheduled to begin on February 9, 1937,
to mark the first anniversary of Kaganovich's momentous visit.[16]

As usual, Bergelson was also engaged in the making of a Yiddish literary journal—this time, a party-funded quarterly called *Forpost*. Its editorial board included six other people, Moyshe Litvakov of the Yevsektsia

among them. Fifteen hundred copies of the first issue came out in July 1936. Eighty-four pages long, it opened with Khavkin's version of the Jewish Autonomous Region's "first two years"—this much time had passed since its official status was granted—and continued with Bergelson's fiction, poetry by Markish, Kazakevich, and others, and essays on the issues of Jewish statehood and the flora and fauna of Birobidzhan.[17]

In August 1936, Chairman Liberberg was suddenly summoned to Moscow.[18] In November, the Kaganovich State Jewish Theater of Birobidzhan hosted a literary evening devoted to the publication of the second issue of *Forpost*. Bergelson attended, of course.[19] The new issue contained works of fiction and poetry, one essay titled "Birobidzhan in Fiction" and another titled "Birobidzhan in Art,"[20] and a notice informing readers that Joseph Liberberg had been "unmasked as untrustworthy, counterrevolutionary, and a bourgeois-nationalist."[21] The Great Terror was beginning, and its first wave of purges would profoundly affect Birobidzhan.

Yiddish-language activists began disappearing in Moscow first. Their organizations—including the daily paper *Der emes*—were being shut down. Bergelson's instincts had once again proved infallible: having established a residence in Birobidzhan allowed him now to watch the purges from afar and act to try to protect himself. In January 1937, he sent a letter to *Literaturnaya gazeta*, the Russian-language Moscow writers' paper, denouncing the Yiddish-language writers who had been arrested[22]—including his former rival and quasi-friend Moyshe Litvakov, who had presided over the public flogging that had been Bergelson's repatriation ritual. Now Litvakov, among others, stood accused of conspiring to create a murderous "Bundist Nazi-Fascist organization"; he confessed to everything and more, even "admitting" membership in the Gestapo.[23] The physical and rhetorical distance Bergelson had put between himself and Litvakov proved life-saving this time.

In March 1937, Bergelson got word that the Yiddish conference he had been planning for late May would be postponed. He recognized the postponement for the cancellation it was, possibly a prelude to arrests of the organizers, so he packed and left Birobidzhan hastily.[24] So did the young Kazakevich—warned, legend has it, by a well-placed friend.[25] Bergelson might have been that friend: he was not well placed in the conventional sense, but his survival instincts were unparalleled.

Liberberg was executed the following month.[26] Bergelson's friend Khavkin was arrested along with his wife; their two children became wards of the state.[27] Waves of arrests swept through the Jewish Autonomous Region: the party was beheaded, the foreigners' collective farm was disbanded, and the entire ethnic Korean population of forty-five hundred was deported to Central Asia in sealed train cars in September 1937.[28] Other ethnic groups living in border regions were similarly moved inland; Stalin had come to view as a vulnerability any ethnic group with potential allegiances to a foreign government. The Jews, of course, had no country besides the Soviet Union to call their own, but building an autonomy near the border now looked like possible treason.[29]

Random arrests are a necessary component of mass terror, and this was true in Birobidzhan. The party elite was targeted disproportionately, but anyone could have been reported by anyone else for saying the wrong thing or looking the wrong way, whether the account was true or not. The chairman of the Trevoga ("Alert") collective farm was sentenced to twenty-five years of exile in Kazakhstan for espionage for Japan;[30] a prominent athlete sent by Moscow to help set up a sports infrastructure in Birobidzhan was arrested on suspicion of being an escaped prisoner and held for nearly two years;[31] a teachers' college student was arrested and never returned;[32] a veterinarian was sentenced to ten years' imprisonment for allegedly poisoning cattle;[33] a woodworker employed by the bathhouse was sentenced to death for allegedly sabotaging the Komsomol in the region, ostensibly on Khavkin's orders.[34] The arrests worked like a fine-toothed comb, sweeping through the villages of the region. One of the oldest living residents of Valdheym, Sima Kogan, told a local amateur historian that she was delivering milk one morning to a house she visited every day "and saw that the house was locked up and the son was sitting on the porch, crying, and she asked why the house was locked up and the boy said that his parents had been arrested in the night and he would now have to go to an orphanage and later he hanged himself."[35]

Khavkin was accused of Trotskyism, "bourgeois nationalism," and counterrevolutionary activities and eventually sentenced to fifteen years in labor camps.[36] His wife, Sofia, was accused of having tried to kill Kaganovich by poisoning him with the gefilte fish he had so highly praised after visiting the Khavkins a year earlier. She spent years in labor camps in Kazakhstan and, upon release, was committed to a psychiatric hospital, where she died.[37]

Bergelson walked a tightrope. In late 1937 the Moscow Yiddish-language journal *Tribuna*, published by OZET, the Committee for the Settlement of Toiling Jews on the Land, labeled him a "professional sycophant"—an apparent reference to his relationship with the disgraced Khavkin. His name disappeared from *Forpost*'s masthead.[38] Bergelson went very, very quiet, as though trying to disappear in plain sight. As did, for now, the whole Jewish autonomy project. OZET and its sister organization, KOMZET, were shut down, taking with them not only the *Tribuna* but also the entire resettlement program, including its system of recruitment centers, chartered trains, and, most important, funding for resettlement, such as it was.[39] Stalin's newfound fear of foreigners in the Soviet midst occasioned the reversal of Soviet nationalities policy: "national" local councils ceased to exist; many non-Russian-language schools closed; the Jewish autonomy project froze.

Birobidzhan reshaped itself. The percentage of Jews in the region's population stood at eighteen. The days of struggling to assimilate hundreds and thousands of new arrivals were over; the rallies, plays, and gala evenings brimming with proud propaganda had ended; the idea of achieving national-republic status had been buried. The local stars were gone: imprisoned or executed, like Khavkin and Liberberg, or escaped into hiding like Bergelson and Kazakevich. The Yiddish-language *Birobidzhaner shtern* had been merged with Russian-language *Birobidzhanskaya zvezda*, similarly eviscerated by the purges. The printing plant, recently outfitted with equipment donated by American Jews, was working at partial capacity.[40] Still, in 1939, the Birobidzhan publishing house put out a book of ABCs in Yiddish[41] and was readying a set of Yiddish-language textbooks for the upper classes, as well as a Russian-Yiddish dictionary, intended to facilitate communication between old and new settlers.[42] The same year, a propaganda booklet authored jointly by Bergelson and the young Kazakevich—presumably written before the purges began—was published for distribution to Jews outside the Soviet Union who might consider moving to the Jewish Autonomous Region. The following year, Birobidzhan held a series of celebrations to honor thirty years of Bergelson's writing career, including a gala event at which excerpts from his work were staged by the Kaganovich State Jewish Theater. Bergelson chose not to come to Birobidzhan for the festivities.[43] Whether these echoes of the earlier state-building efforts were the product of inertia or a new, ominous change in policy is not clear.

On August 23, 1939, the Soviet Union and Nazi Germany signed a nonaggression treaty that has become known as the Molotov-Ribbentrop Pact, after the two foreign ministers who brokered the deal. According to the document, the Soviet Union would colonize two Baltic states—Estonia and Latvia—as well as parts of Finland, Poland, and Romania. Germany would take Lithuania, among other lands. The provisions for the territorial division, however, were kept secret, and only the nonaggression part of the treaty was publicized.[1] Those who lived in the countries squeezed between Germany and the Soviet Union were left to wonder at what cost and on what premises the two giants had promised peace to each other.

On September 1, 1939, Germany invaded Poland. On September 3, Britain, France, New Zealand, and Australia declared war on Germany. On September 5, the United States proclaimed neutrality. On September 17, with most of Poland in German hands, the Soviet Union invaded the country from the east. On September 29, the USSR and Germany formalized their partition of Poland. The Soviet Union thus acquired hundreds of thousands of new Jewish citizens, many of them politically active. The troublemakers needed to be moved out of the way, and Birobidzhan was an obvious option. In 1940, a group of Moscow officials visited Birobidzhan to investigate the possibility of resettling the Jews of Poland in the Jewish Autonomous Region.[2] The authorities ultimately chose the more traditional option, however, and Polish Jews were either imprisoned or exiled, mostly to Siberia. My great-grandmother, a Bundist from Białystok, was among them.

Bergelson, who had watched Hitler's rise in Berlin, who had picked a lesser evil when he'd opted for Moscow, had to be frightfully pained by the new alliance. All evidence indicates, however, that he continued to keep very quiet. His old acquaintance and fellow repatriate Perets Markish was not quite as careful. Dispatched to occupied Białystok to convert Yiddish writers to Soviet ways, Markish showed an old friend an article written by an American. The author had been a Communist sympathizer until the Stalin-Hitler pact had shown him that "he raised a snake around his neck." Commented Markish, "Only he nourished this snake around his neck? Only he alone? And maybe all of us weaned the snake? And a time may come when this full-grown snake will choke all of us. . . . Yes, if it keeps going like it's been going, the time will come that the snake wrapped around our necks will choke us."[3]

Markish then broke down crying and, when he had calmed, begged his friend to keep quiet about the conversation—a request the friend respected for two decades. Markish returned to Moscow and began writing a heartbreaking poem called "The Dancer from the Ghetto," while an epic poem glorifying Stalin, written before the pact, was published, as though to protect him.[4]

The Yiddish Soviet writers were wrapped tightly in the snake's embrace. Bergelson knew much more than most Soviet citizens. The whole world could be claiming ignorance for years to come, but Bergelson could distinguish the finest hues of threat. He had seen the raw animal hatred that turned all of Germany, and the people it occupied, into armies of murderers. He had heard enough about the ghettos to know that in them Jews would be humiliated, disgraced, and ultimately killed by the hundreds of thousands. And he knew that for nearly fifteen years he had willingly and willfully stayed in the propaganda service of a state that had not only murdered some of his friends but was now, through its new alliance with Germany, enabling the murder of his people. If Bergelson wanted to stay alive, if he wanted his wife and son to be safe, he had to silence the despair welling up in his throat, he had to hold back his tears of outrage, and he had to keep his hands from putting pen to paper, even if it felt like his people's last chance to cry for help.

For now, the Baltic states remained technically unoccupied (though they were coming under increased political pressure from the Soviet Union), and Dubnow, in Riga, chose to interpret his location as wisely chosen. On October 9, less than two weeks after the German-Soviet partition of Poland, he wrote in a letter, "What has happened is what we feared, so psychologically, we were prepared. . . . We have been worried strongly here, though we are living in a neutral country. At first we feared that these small countries would be smashed between giants, but recently we have been reassured: the sovereignty of the Baltic states is certain. I have therefore decided to decline my American friends' offer to make the move across the ocean. It would have upset my spiritual equilibrium, which is all the more essential at times like these. . . . I am especially worried now about the fate of my children in Warsaw."[5]

Latvia's fate had been sealed two months earlier. Sovereignty would be forfeited in less than a year, in July 1940, when the Soviet Union took the Baltics. Earlier in the year, the Soviet Union had secured its hold over a chunk of Finland, and Germany had taken Denmark, Norway, France, Belgium, Luxembourg, and the Netherlands. In another eleven months, on June 22, 1941, Germany would break the nonaggression pact and invade the USSR, consolidating what it had grabbed in Europe and quickly advancing east.

On October 25, 1941, the Jews of Riga were ordered to move into the ghetto. Less than two months later, most of them—about twenty-four thousand—were marched to the Rumbula Forest, outside the city, and shot there.[6] According to the story established after the war was over, Dubnow was still in the city on December 8, the last day of the Rumbula massacre. He was, his biographer wrote in the 1950s, ordered onto a bus that would presumably have taken him to the forest, but the eighty-one-year-old historian, who had been ill and was running a fever, did not move fast enough, so one of the German soldiers shot him right in the city street.[7] In fact, there were no buses: the Jews of Riga had to march to their death, and uncounted hundreds of those who were too slow died or were killed en route.[8] Dubnow must have been among them.

The man who had spent decades thinking and writing about Jewish emigration had not known when to run, or where. Or had he? Dubnow had known to flee Berlin. He had spent six or seven peaceful years in Latvia. His October 1939 letter reassuring his friends, and himself, that Riga was a safe place reads tragically wrong seventy-six years later—especially now, as I write this, when Riga has become a safe haven for my friends escaping the Putin regime in Russia, and I worry about the wisdom of their choice—but then I find myself coming back, over and over, to the two years and two months that passed between that letter and Dubnow's death. From the vantage point of my current secure middle age in America, these two years look negligible, a footnote to Dubnow's larger error, but these were two years that the Jews in the German-occupied part of Poland spent subsisting and dying in the ghettos. These were two years that Dubnow would not have lived had he stayed in Berlin. These were two years during which many of his friends who had made a home or sought refuge elsewhere found themselves under Nazi occupation—including the friends to whom he wrote that 1939 letter. They lived in Paris, which German troops occupied in June 1940. On June 23, Hitler toured Paris. Soviet troops took Riga exactly one month later, and to many Latvian Jews, their presence seemed to promise security.

Only if I zoom in on those two years do I realize that for months at a time life must have felt stable—stable enough, at least, for Dubnow to consider his options in the tiny part of Europe he had chosen. "I have found myself recently taken with the thoughts of emigration," Dubnow wrote to his Paris friends in December 1939. "I am not speaking of America, though my friends there have secured a visa for me and it has been waiting at the American consul's office for over a month. I have decided that in the spring I shall move to Lithuania, either to Wilna or to Kowno." He was using the Polish transcription of cities now known as Vilnius and Kaunas—two intellectual and cultural centers of Lithuanian and Polish Jewry that had bounced between Poland and Lithuania and within the Russia Empire but were not, for the moment, occupied by Germany. Among other things, Dubnow wrote, he hoped he could work to strengthen YIVO if he moved to Wilna.

He reassured his friends that he was being watchful and cautious. "If the circumstances change and it turns out that my being in the Baltics contains some risks," he wrote, "then I shall make use of the American visa, for an extension of which I intend to petition the consulate. Let's hope, however, that the situation will improve and we shall yet see a free Europe."

Dubnow was concerned that the British and their allies—which did not yet include the United States, still formally neutral—were not sufficiently aware of the damage done to Jewish communities, especially in Poland, then the civilizational center of world Jewry. "We must create a periodical, either in London or in Paris, for exchanging views on the role of the Jewry in the world war," he wrote. "My plan is as follows: first, we must collect information for a 'Black Book' that would reflect the looting of our center in Poland; second, we should begin publishing a weekly devoted to the role of the Jewry in the time of war and in the future 'new Europe.' Both the book and the newspaper should be published in English in consideration of the outside world and the millions of English-speaking Jews in America. . . . I have written a letter to the editor of 'The Times' saying that the goals of the war must be expanded to include not only [the liberation of] Poland, Czechoslovakia, etc., but also the restoration of devastated Jewish centers on which Hitler has declared the most ruthless of wars."

The word "ruthless," as used by Dubnow in 1939, supposed that there would remain something to be restored, someone to do the restoring, and someone to document the destruction. He had perhaps a deeper understanding of Jewish life and identity than anyone before or after him, but the tragedy that was about to befall the Jews would have required an impossible imagination to be able to conjure it.

Dubnow had to scrap his plan to move to Lithuania after the Soviet invasion: the borders between newly occupied Soviet territories were sealed shut. His closest friends had fled Paris for the South of France, where they were desperately working to get a visa that could be used to escape. Dubnow tried to inquire about the status of his United States visa, but he could learn nothing. The only news he received from the outside world came in the form of magazines occasionally arriving from Palestine. But he did not hear from his old Odessa friends who had made their way to Palestine and who were managing his savings, which he had seen fit to deposit there. He was eighty-one years old, widowed, alone, and isolated in a city that had never felt like his own.

"During a time of anxiety twenty years ago, I was living in my homeland and hoping to leave for Berlin in a year," he recalled in a letter. "Now I am not going anywhere: all roads are blocked off. Berlin has turned into Sodom, and all our European centers have been destroyed by the Sodomites. America and Palestine are looking at me from the opposite ends of the earth, and I set my sights on them too. But I know that they are unreachable and I am doomed to remain in this 'vast and fearful desert.'"9 The great secular thinker was quoting Deuteronomy, the final book of the Tanakh, in which Moses tells the Jews that if they obey God's law, they will not be harmed by the people who live across the Jordan River.

As for his "children in Warsaw," Dubnow was, of course, right to worry about them. His oldest daughter, Sofia, moved to Vilnius with her family, but her husband, the Bund leader Henryk Erlich, was arrested by the Soviets. He and another Bund leader, Wiktor Alter, were tried and sentenced to death, though their sentences were then reduced to ten years of hard labor. Sofia Dubnova-Erlich ran. Her husband was in a Soviet prison, her father was effectively being held prisoner by the Soviets, and yet she ran, with her two grown sons, first to Japan, then to Canada, and finally to New York. Her older son became an economist; he studied Soviet economics and taught at Columbia University. Her younger son served in the U.S. Army and later headed the Russian department at Yale. Their mother had been brought up right—to run, when one must, without looking back.

Within weeks of breaking the nonaggression pact, Germany had taken eastern Poland, Belarus, and Ukraine, the areas that still had the Soviet Union's largest Jewish population. Nazi troops were marching toward Moscow almost as fast as their feet could carry them, so ineffectual was the Red Army's resistance. In the face of the coming catastrophe, Bergelson was about to get his voice back.

Six weeks after the German invasion, Solomon Lozovsky, the Jewish deputy chairman of the Soviet Information Bureau (Sovinformburo), the state news monopoly, received a letter signed by eight prominent Jews. They included Bergelson, Kvitko, and Markish as well as the great actor Solomon Mikhoels and a highly decorated poet named Itsik Fefer. The letter proposed "to organize a Jewish rally aimed at the Jews of the USA and great Britain but also at Jews in other countries." It emphasized that "a rally with the participation of Jewish academicians, writers, artists, and Red Army fighters will have a great impact abroad."[1] It included a list of twelve proposed speakers, fourth among them "D. Bergelson, the great Jewish writer."[2] Bergelson was offering to do for the state what he had done so well before: sell Soviet needs to rich foreign Jews. It would be a fund-raiser for the Soviet war effort.

On August 24, 1941, thousands of people gathered in Gorky Park in central Moscow to listen to Bergelson and his comrades, led by Mikhoels. The war, it seemed, had lifted the ban on speaking as Jews—not Soviet Jews, not toiling-on-the-land Jews, but Jews who had a history before the revolution, Jews who had been raised reading the Torah, Jews who no longer had anything to fear, because Hitler's advancing army was within weeks of reaching Moscow.

The Soviet ban on religious speech had relaxed in the early days of the war, when the Red Army command spontaneously began to rely on clergy—what little remained of it after the years of terror—to pull together and inspire the troops. It is not clear that Bergelson knew this; rather, he, Markish, and the others might have reached for religious speech the way human beings reach for ritual when they experience overwhelming fear. Speaking at the rally, Markish invoked the image of "the biblical Job, stunned by everything that passed before his eyes." The writer Ilya Ehrenburg, another returned émigré, now on his way to becoming the country's single most influential journalist, said, "I grew up in a Russian city. My mother tongue is Russian. I am a Russian writer. Like all Russians, I am now defending my homeland. But the Nazis have reminded me of something else; my mother's name was Hannah. I am a Jew. I say this proudly. Hitler hates us more than anything, and this makes us proud."[3]

Bergelson spoke in Yiddish. "Dear brothers and sisters," he said, as a statesman would say addressing the people he led, as, indeed, Stalin had said at the start of his first speech after the German invasion.[4] "Jews of the whole world . . . It is also [Hitler's] plan to wipe out all peoples, and in the first place, the Jewish people. . . . The bandit Hitler makes no distinction between workers and manufacturers, between freethinkers and religious people, between assimilated and unassimilated Jews." Whom was he addressing? American Jews, who needed to hear that Soviet Jews were Jews, too, even if they had for twenty years been "scratching off their own Jewishness until blood starts to run," as he had written in *Forverts*? Soviet Jews, who needed to hear that their plight was shared by millions? Himself, because he needed to sound out the line from Psalm 118 that he had used to title his speech: "I shall not die, but live"?[5] Emboldened by despair, or perhaps sensing that exhibiting a little liberty would go a long way toward making his appeal effective abroad, he said the words in Hebrew, a language banned by Soviet law nearly twenty years earlier.

For all people of occupied countries, Hitlerism means slavery, persecution, and torture; for us Jews, though, it means total extermination and the end. The question of survival becomes absolutely clear. It concerns life or death for our people. . . . Vandalizing Fascism still rages. It destroys everything, and we Jews will be the first to be thrown into the fire. Our people, though, will not perish . . . the people who, thousands of years ago, proudly told its tormentors, *Lo amut ki ekhye*, "I shall not die, but live."[6]

Sovinformburo organized a radio broadcast of the rally to allied countries and distributed an additional document titled "An Appeal to World Jewry." Bergelson was almost certainly one of its primary authors.

Fellow Jews the world over!

While the murderous fascists have brought a "new order" to the enslaved countries with the aid of the knife, the gallows, fire and violence, Hitler's bloody regime has brutally planned the complete and unconditional annihilation of the Jewish people by all means available to the fascist executioners.

In Poland alone, Hitler's men have tortured and murdered more than three million Poles and Jews in the most savage and shameless way, raped daughters in front of their parents and smashed the heads of children in the presence of their mothers. . . .

Fellow Jews! As history fatefully willed it, the Jewish people, dispersed throughout the entire world, linked their own culture closely to the culture of peoples all over the world.

In those countries seized and enslaved by fascism, our unfortunate brothers have become the first victims. The blood of Jews tortured in the burning synagogues of Rotterdam calls out to the entire world, as do the thousands of unmarked graves in the towns and villages of Poland, in which the fascist barbarians buried their victims alive.

The spilled blood demands not fasting and prayers, but revenge!

It is not by memorial candles but by fire that the murderers of humanity must be destroyed. Not tears, but hate and resistance to the monsters and beasts! Not words but deeds! It's now or never![7]

The way the story is told to this day, back in 1941, no one knew. Even at Adolf Eichmann's trial in Jerusalem in 1961, there was argument about who among the Nazi leadership had learned of plans for a "final solution" and at which point, and the entire year of 1941 was contested territory.[8] The people who wrote this address knew. Nothing—not the Iron Curtain or the willful ignorance of the world's Jews—could shield them from the knowledge, for Hitler had told them all they needed to know back in January 1939, when news from Germany was still being reported in the Soviet press. In a speech at the Reichstag back then, Hitler had predicted that there would be a war that would bring about "the annihilation of the Jewish race in Europe."[9]

Few people wanted to know. It appears that only the New York Yiddish dailies picked up the appeal, distributed in the United States by the Jewish Telegraphic Agency. This might have been only the second time they carried reports of the killing of Jews in Eastern Europe, the first having appeared in July of that year, when they wrote that hundreds of Jews had been massacred by Germans in the occupied territories of Ukraine and Belarus. The *New York Times* would not acknowledge this information until October 1941—and it was not until at least spring 1942 that a prominent report finally appeared in the *Times*.[10] By this time, Poland, Ukraine, Belarus, and the Baltic states—those parts of Europe that were home to the largest number of Jews—had been under German occupation for between seven months and two and a half years.

Three weeks after the rally, German troops took Kyiv, the city Bergelson probably still loved more than any place he had lived. Many of the non-Jewish residents of the city—and, who knows, perhaps some of the Jews as well—welcomed the Germans, who had showered the city with flyers in advance of their arrival, promising an end to the Soviet regime and a life of order and plenty. In five days, Khreshchatyk, Kyiv's majestic central avenue, went up in flames, following a series of explosions of mines apparently planted by the Soviets before they abandoned the city without a fight; most of those killed were civilians. In another two weeks, Nazi troops marched between thirty and seventy thousand Jews, in groups one after another, to a ravine on the outskirts of the city, ordered them to strip naked, opened machine-gun fire on them, and then quickly covered up the ravine, while some of the victims were still alive.[11] This method of massacre would be reproduced repeatedly throughout Ukraine and the Baltics, in all the shtetlach, whose names Bergelson still knew by heart.

In October 1941, panic broke out in Moscow. All hope that the city could be protected was lost; people fled by train if they were lucky, by car, horse-drawn cart, and even by foot if they were not. They took only what they could carry, and they disposed of anything they felt might endanger them, like books on Marxism, party documents, Soviet uniforms—the streets were littered with the skin Soviet people had shed, fleeing. As a newly reintegrated member of the Soviet propaganda establishment, Bergelson was able to leave Moscow during a partial evacuation; he went to the old Volga city of Kuybyshev, where a temporary capital was being set up.

In the middle of all this, he wrote a play called *Kh'vel lebn* (I will live), set in the present, in a town facing Hitler's advancing troops. One of the characters considers suicide. The wise old man character, Avraham-Ber, admonishes him, "We, the ordinary Jews, have seen many dead people in our lives. . . . Yet the more they multiply, the greater our desire to live. . . . They did not commit suicide. . . . They did not stop proclaiming, 'I shall not die but will live.' "[12]

More important, he wrote letters. In addition to proposing the rally, Bergelson and the seven other famous Soviet Jews offered to create a committee that would mobilize the world's Jewry to aid the Soviet Union in fighting Hitler and starting a newspaper. "The Jewish press of Minsk, Kovno, Vilnius, Lvov, Białystok and a number of other cities has ceased to exist," they wrote to Lozovsky. "We therefore raise before the Soviet Information Bureau the question of the urgent need to establish a Yiddish newspaper. There are sufficient literary personnel as well as printing facilities in Moscow to maintain such a newspaper. A Yiddish newspaper in Moscow will play a major role in organizing the Jewish masses for the support of our homeland."[13] These letters went unheeded. Meanwhile, the Jews of Ukraine were packing their bags and appearing in the designated public squares of their cities and towns at the appointed hour, apparently unaware not only that they would now be marched to a ravine and executed but even that they had particular reason to fear the Nazis.[14] All Bergelson could do to counteract this was write a brochure for Soviet Jews, published by *Der emes* in Moscow in the fall of 1941. "The human imagination is too limited to paint a picture of the atrocities they have thought up," he wrote. "Haman was nothing but a dog compared to them."[15]

12

In the spring of 1942, the Communist Party gave its official permission for the founding of the Jewish Anti-Fascist Committee, with Mikhoels as chair. Mikhoels and Fefer would travel to the United States to personally raise funds. Even the Polish Bund leaders Erlich—Dubnow's son-in-law—and Alter, who were famous among the Jewish American Left, had been released from prison at the end of the previous year, in preparation for this effort. Soon after the work began, however, they disappeared from view. In 1943, the Soviet Union acknowledged that both were dead; they were understood to have been executed, although years later it emerged that Erlich had committed suicide in his jail cell in May 1942, some time after Alter was executed. The news of the deaths, first reported by the *New Republic* in early 1943, caused an outrage and even calls for a total boycott of the Soviet Union, but soon was forgotten. Sofia Dubnova-Erlich learned both of her husband's and her father's deaths only after she had arrived in New York following a year-long journey.

The JAC would have a newspaper, published every ten days, to be called *Eynikayt* (Unity) and to be run by an editorial board of five, including Bergelson, Mikhoels, and Kvitko. It was at *Eynikayt* that Bergelson finally found the journalistic voice that he and others had for so long demanded from him, back when all he seemed capable of producing came out shrill, as when he wrote his anti-Soviet diatribes for *Forverts*, or stilted, as when he turned pro-Soviet. Now he was fighting for the survival of his people.

Bergelson's first essay for *Eynikayt* was called "May the World Be a Witness."

May the world bear witness that the following will take place. The Jewish people once created a book that, for thousands of years, has been read more than any other book. That same Jewish people will find within itself sufficient strength to create a book that, for thousands of years, will tell the world about fascist atrocities everywhere, in every corner of every country where the Nazi jackboots have trampled.[1]

Simon Dubnow, who may have been the first to suggest the idea of a book—*The Black Book*—that would document Nazi crimes against the Jews, had been dead almost a year when Bergelson set out to tell the story of the Holocaust in his articles. His first one, published in September 1942, was called "Gedenkt" (Remember) and related the story of the Jews of Vitebsk, who were massacred on October 8, 1941. He kept at it, looking for and finding ways to write something beyond a litany of losses, feeling his way to creating something like a dirge, a text that could convey the full weight of what was being killed: an entire world.

On May Day 1943, he published an homage to Kyiv, then still under German occupation:

From high up on Khreshtchatik one can descend all the way down to Podol. It is better to go on foot rather than to drive. On the right, at the very edge of the hill's peak, the tram-car goes up and down, like a rhythmic, creeping funicular. A bit farther away you can see the Dnieper playing with its depths. An old river, perhaps even greying a little, it seems, but none the less still playful. It plays with the sun on hot summer days. It plays with the storm-clouds in late autumn. It plays with ships and barges that glide over it, and it plays with all the smallest splinters that skip along its waves when it is just beginning to freeze over. It is an old-young river. From its highest of heights and lowest of depths it reflects the image of Kiev, also a playful, old-new city.[2]

It was the city of Bergelson's youth, the city where he had become a man and a writer, the city where his son had been a baby and he himself had careened from mad hope to desperate fear, the city he had escaped with his wife, his son, and his friends. He had traveled the world looking for a home, he seemed to have all but forgotten his Kyiv, but as he neared his sixtieth birthday, the pain of seeing Kyiv destroyed—rather, of having enough information to imagine the destruction with striking clarity—proved searing. He described it now as a Jewish city:

> From the Black Sea to places beyond Kiev, in all cities and towns, every Friday at sunset, at exactly the same hour, at exactly the same minute, at exactly the same instant, Jewish windows were aflame with candlelight.

Under Soviet rule, Kyiv remained a Jewish city. The Germans had killed it. Bergelson wrote of Podol, the poor, filthy Jewish trading area of Kyiv:

> All that's left of Podol are empty ruins. From twisted balconies hang the ropes and nooses of gallows. In a grave near the Jewish hospital lie fifty-six thousand Jews, shot to death or buried alive. In the Goloseyev forest at the edge of Demievka, by the glow of nocturnal fires German soldiers receive their hangman's pay for smashing the heads of hundreds and hundreds of Jewish children against the trunks of trees—for each smashed child's skull, a full glass of schnaps. . . . Oh, Kiev, tortured city, slaughtered but at the same time not slaughtered, on your devastated hills! You will surely be asking, "Where are you now, my children?"[3]

This child was now back in Moscow, apparently torn like never before between his need and desire to do what he could to speak for the Jews of Europe and his shame at being allowed to utter but a few of the words that welled up. The Polish Jewish poet Rokhl Korn, who spent the war years in Russia, working with the Jewish Anti-Fascist Committee, described a heartbreaking scene in Bergelson's home.

He took me by the arm and led me into his study. He stopped in front of his portrait which was hung on the wall and asked: "Do you see him?" I answered: "Yes, who painted it?" being sure he wanted to comment on the painter. But as though he had not heard the question he kept pointing his finger at his own portrait and like one possessed he shouted into my ear: "Look at him, take a good look at him—I hate his guts—the filthy scoundrel!"

Only later did I begin to grasp the full tragedy of this scene. This was David Bergelson's way of turning to the free world and asking that he not be judged too harshly for having given in, and having served a false idolatry both in his work and in his personal life. He realized that he was already a prisoner of Soviet reality but I, who was still a Polish citizen, still had a chance to leave the prison that housed 200 million.[4]

Bergelson turned sixty on August 12, 1944. A public reception was held in Moscow. *Eynikayt* published a special supplement celebrating his contributions to literature and the theater, and in particular—addressing Bergelson in the second person—it lauded him for "your great and wide-ranging anti-fascist activity. With your fiery words you summon the Jewish masses to battle against the accursed enemy of humankind, against the hangman of the Jewish people."[5] Five days after his birthday, *Eynikayt* came out with Bergelson's report on Majdanek—the first death camp to have been liberated, just a month earlier. It was called "The Germans Did This!"

This will be engraved on the memory of humanity for ever. . . .
—In Majdanek!
This is the spit in the face of everyone who feels and thinks and sees in life something rational and good, who believes that it is in man's power to make life better and more beautiful.
—In Majdanek!
. . . Was it only Mafeld and Tuman [who ran the camp] who did this? This is the question each of our Red Army soldiers had to ask

himself when bearing witness to a field strewn with hundreds of thousands of people's shoes, soldiers who were led to see a decaying body killed by an electric current, who were led to . . . [a person] begging, as though for alms, "Please, hang me."

Who can, in such a moment, attempt to work out how many pairs of shoes on that field belonged to Jews, and how many belonged to Poles, to Russians, Ukrainians, Greeks, Frenchmen, Dutchmen, to Norwegians, or to Serbs? We Jews? . . .

Almost to the last person he [the German] exterminated our brothers in the occupied regions. In the places where Polish, Lithuanian, and Latvian Jews used to live and create, all he left behind was vacancy, and with an abandoned cynicism he inscribed into that vacancy:

—Vilna without Jews!

—Kovno without Jews!

—Warsaw without Jews!

And yet we alone do not have the power to gain restitution for our great tragedy, and the plague called "Germans" is not ours alone. It is a plague on the whole world.[6]

In July 1943, *Eynikayt* announced that a single book documenting the killing of European Jews would be created and called on readers to submit their stories; the book would be titled *The Black Book*, just as Dubnow had imagined. Albert Einstein would write one of the introductions. Bergelson's old acquaintance Sholem Asch, who'd once tried to persuade him to emigrate to the United States, would be one of its American editors. The entire Jewish Anti-Fascist Committee and several other prominent Russian Jewish writers would take part. The Soviet Union's most popular journalist and Bergelson's fellow wandering Jew Ilya Ehrenburg would be the editor. It would be a book for reading, a book of heart-rending stories rather than a collection of documents. "This book cannot be good or bad," Ehrenburg wrote at the time. "We are not writing it; the Nazis are."[7]

The book was to be published in eleven languages. The world would know. The manuscript was completed in early 1944.[8] The censorship process commenced. Einstein's introduction had to be dropped because he wrote that the Jews, through their suffering, had earned the right to their own nation-state.[9] Parts of the book were published in 1945–46 in the United States and in Romania,[10] but the definitive Russian-language edition, titled *The Black Book of the Evil and Commonplace Killing of the Jews by the Nazi Occupiers in the Temporarily Occupied Lands of the Soviet Union and in Hitlerite Death Camps on Polish Territory During the War of 1941–1945*, languished, designed, typeset, laid out, and unpublished. Times had changed once again. Not only were the Jews no longer needed to organize international support for the war effort; in the new postwar disposition they had become more suspect than they had ever been before. As represented by the JAC, they had had unprecedented contact with foreigners during the war years. In addition, with the founding, in 1948, of the State of Israel, the Jews, in Stalin's eyes, became, like the other minority nations of the Soviet Union, potentially allied with a foreign power. They became internal enemies.

13

Within two years of the war's end, the project of forgetting it commenced. Victory Day, which had briefly been an official holiday, became just another day. War veterans were stripped of the benefits they had been granted. Those who had been maimed were rounded up and sent to places where they would not serve as living reminders of the carnage. Cultural production about the war halted. Bergelson, too, stopped writing about the war—in addition to his articles, he had written two plays, *Kh'vel lebn* (I will live) and *Prints Ruveni* (Prince Reuveni, the story of a sixteenth-century false messiah who calls on the Jews to take up arms), and now he turned, once again, to the story of Birobidzhan. He picked up the narrative of a disoriented American Jew pursuing false capitalist ideals in the socialist Eden in the Far East. It was as lifeless as his previous writing on Birobidzhan.

Of the roughly five million Soviet Jews, half had been murdered; perhaps as many as half of the rest had been displaced. Throughout Ukraine and Belarus, German troops had rounded up and, in most cases, killed the Jews in the first weeks after the invasion; over the two to three years of occupation that followed, Jewish homes, entire neighborhoods, and whole settlements had been colonized by the non-Jews, for whom the opportunity to claim additional living space had been one of the few benefits of German rule. At the end of the war, the lucky survivors among Soviet Jews faced the prospect of returning to homes that were no longer theirs, occupied by strangers or former neighbors and surrounded by the memory and, literally, the remains of loved ones they had left behind. Two groups of people—Stalin's government, on the one hand, and JAC activists and their American allies, on the other—realized this long before the displaced Jews themselves knew of their predicament. Both the Soviet government and the Jewish activists understood that allowing the Jews of Ukraine and Belarus to return to what they thought was home would be a disaster.

There was the idea of resettling the Jews in the Crimea. It seems to have been born—or, rather, reborn, for this had been tried already, before the founding of Birobidzhan—during Mikhoels's and Itsik Fefer's fundraising trip to the United States, on behalf of the JAC, in 1943. They apparently ran their idea by the Kremlin and, thinking it vetted, wrote letters to Stalin and foreign minister Molotov, urging "the formation of a Soviet Jewish republic [that] would solve once and for all in a Bolshevik manner, in the spirit of the Leninist-Stalinist nationalities policy, the problem of the state and legal position of the Jewish people and the further development of its long-lived culture. Such a problem, which was impossible to solve for many centuries, can be solved only in our Great Socialist country."[1] In keeping with the Soviet tradition of obliterating history, the letter pretended that neither Birobidzhan nor the earlier Crimean experiment had existed.

Kvitko was dispatched to the Crimea on a reconnaissance mission. It was as if everyone had forgotten that the Soviet Union had already solved the Jewish problem in full accordance with Leninist-Stalinist nationalities policy, by settling the Jews on the border with China. Everyone, that is, but Lazar Kaganovich, who once summoned several JAC members to rebuke them for the Crimea plan.[2] The incident apparently did not frighten the others, but it must have had particular resonance for Bergelson. His last contact with Kaganovich had concerned the ill-fated Yiddish-language conference in Birobidzhan, which Kaganovich had inspired and which would have landed Bergelson in jail had he persisted in trying to organize it. This was the man who'd praised the Khavkins' hospitality and home cooking and later ruined their lives by accusing them of trying to poison him. Bergelson knew enough not to take part in the Crimea project. He turned to Birobidzhan, though he never again returned there.

In February 1944, the JAC convened a meeting in Moscow devoted to the future of Soviet Jewry, which represented the absolute majority of the surviving Jews of Europe. The Crimea proposal figured most prominently. But a representative from Birobidzhan argued, as a participant recalled, that "despite all its past failures and difficulties, this was a propitious time to develop Birobidzhan." Ilya Ehrenburg, the celebrated novelist and war correspondent, was outraged: "You people are trying to create a new ghetto!" In 1944, this was quite a grave accusation. A Yiddish poet recalled that Bergelson "expressed enthusiasm for its natural beauty and its wealth of resources. 'A Jewish writer, especially a poet,' he assured me, 'will find much there to inspire him.'" Markish was more circumspect, noting that "it's so far away from everything!"[3]

The Jews started coming to Birobidzhan. Some came alone or in pairs, shards of families killed by the Nazis, lone remnants of communities that had been destroyed. Sometimes they were young men who had survived the war as soldiers only to find out that everyone they had known was dead. More often, they were young widows with children, women who had lost their husbands at the front and everyone else back home. They were also children orphaned by the war, collected in the ruins of Jewish Eastern Europe and shipped all the way to Birobidzhan to grow up alongside others of their kind. An American Jewish charitable organization donated the money to start an orphanage.

The children were housed in one of the two-story wooden barracks that made up most of the city of Birobidzhan now. It was staffed entirely with Yiddish-speaking teachers, tender aging Jewish mothers led by Matvey Khazansky, a Red Army officer who had been injured in the war but managed to march into Berlin with his troops. Nicknamed Mota by the kids, he was a patriot of Birobidzhan, one of the old breed who dreamed of a mini-state with Yiddish as its official language, and a devout Communist. He managed to fit a twelve-foot portrait of Stalin into the building.

Whenever the Jewish orphans wanted to be really, truly, totally believed, they said, "I give you my word, for the sake of Lenin, Stalin, and all our great leaders." Mota was as tough a taskmaster as the great leader he adored. Misbehavior such as cutting classes at the Yiddish-language school was punished with ten lashes of a soldier's wide leather belt. School-age children had to contribute to running the house by performing such tasks as splitting frozen coal apart with an ice pick or getting water from the well in any weather, including the kind of regular winter weather in which hands froze to the metal handle even through mittens.[4]

It had been a decade since purges had devastated the autonomist project. Israel Emiot, a Polish Yiddish poet who had survived the war in Siberia, now arrived to be the new bard of Birobidzhan—in essence, to take over Bergelson's old job. He described what he found: "The Jewish cultural situation was lamentable, to say the least. The only Yiddish newspaper there had been shut down by decree during the war. Only one Russian daily—with an occasional Yiddish page—was being published. The whole thing was most painful. The Yiddish typecases in the print shop were full, expert Yiddish typesetters were walking around idle, and no Yiddish publications were being printed." Birobidzhan was a shadow of the illusion it had once been. The Yiddish theater founded by Kazakevich was still functioning, though Kazakevich himself had moved to Moscow in 1938. There was a Yiddish secondary school, where, Emiot wrote, "Jewish youngsters could be heard fervently reciting the words of Mendele, Peretz, Sholem Aleichem, Bergelson, Hofshtein, and other writers. But the official language of the region was no longer Yiddish, as it had been in 1936, when the courts, the police department, the city administration, and various other official activities were conducted in that language. The Pedagogical Institute, which until 1937 had a department for training Yiddish elementary grade teachers, was closed."

Still, Emiot, for one, found reasons for pride and hope. A couple of Bauhaus buildings had been constructed before those plans were scrapped—the hospital and the theater—and new Jewish doctors and Jewish actors were now arriving in the region. "There were definite signs of a revival," he noted. "Early in 1945 a Yiddish anthology was published. The Yiddish theater showed evidence of new life. Several local Yiddish playwrights were writing for the theater's repertoire. . . . More Yiddish writers had come to settle. There was talk of opening a Yiddish college." Most of all, Emiot noticed that Birobidzhan was apparently immune to the anti-Semitic resurgence in other parts of the Soviet Union. "A Jew could still feel at home in Birobidzhan. . . . I recall an incident where one such character got drunk and in broad daylight began bellowing, '*Bey zhidov!* Beat the kikes!' In no time he was surrounded by a crowd of Jewish war invalids who took off his coat and whacked him so unmercifully that he had a miraculous change of heart. '*Lyublyu yevreyev!* I love the Jews!' he protested. The Jews of Birobidzhan did not hesitate to use their fists to answer anti-Semitic slurs."

The schoolchildren had their own choir, which performed songs in Yiddish; they were known all the way to Khabarovsk for their uniforms: bright white shirts with pants and bows of red velvet, courtesy of the American charities that seemed to be showering Birobidzhan with gifts.[5] A small group of writers and poets was starting a new literary journal in Yiddish, to be called *Birobidzhan*. The group revolved around Lyubov Vasserman, a poet who had been born dirt-poor in Poland; had still been a teenager when she emigrated to Palestine, where she worked as a domestic and was arrested as a subversive; and had finally settled in Birobidzhan. (She was one of the young poets who had so charmed Bergelson during a hike when he had first visited Birobidzhan.) Her husband, Moshe Bengelsdorf, had come from Argentina; he worked at the Jewish theater.[6] The journal's planning meetings were held at their apartment.

Transports of new settlers were arriving almost daily. Emiot described the way they were greeted: "Jubilant crowds jammed the railroad stations. The city's Young Pioneer groups came to toss fresh flowers at the incoming trains. All the orchestras in the area joined the celebration and played lively Jewish tunes. The eyes of the immigrants brimmed with tears of joy. The new arrivals were put up temporarily in barracks, in private homes. Jews danced in the street. Yiddish writers read their work before gatherings of new immigrants."

Documents preserved in the state archives in Birobidzhan report that hundreds of families were arriving from the Crimea and Ukraine. When I was in Birobidzhan in 2009, I interviewed the man who was perhaps the last surviving voluntary settler in Birobidzhan. Ninety-year-old Iosif Bekerman told me he had been born to an impoverished family in a shtetl in Ukraine. He was in the city of Kharkiv, in eastern Ukraine, studying to be a pharmacist, when the German army marched into Ukraine from the west. Bekerman had suffered a serious injury as a child; when I met him, he was about four foot eleven, his left arm significantly shorter than his right and hanging limply. While he had probably been stronger and taller when he was a young man, during the Soviet war with Germany he had been judged unfit for military service. He was lucky enough to be evacuated and survive far from the front line, in the Urals. When he went home after the war, the locals explained to him that all the Jews of his village had been rounded up in February 1942 and buried in a single pit. "They told me that pit was heaving for days because so many of the people were buried alive," Bekerman said. Only two Jews in the entire village had survived, both of them hidden by Ukrainian peasants; one of them was Bekerman's aunt.

Bekerman returned to Kharkiv to finish his education and to dream of Birobidzhan; he had read about it in the Yiddish-language papers, and he was convinced it was the promised land. He signed up to become a settler as soon as he graduated, and he arrived in Birobidzhan in the summer of 1948. "I asked the head of the pharmaceutical department, I said, 'I wrote you a letter asking to come and you never wrote back, why didn't you write back?' and she said, 'What is good here?' And I knew what she meant, she meant there is nothing good here." He told me of the wooden barracks saturated with the stench of too many human lives crammed together; wooden sidewalks laid right over swampland, its own stench stubbornly seeping through; and the mosquitoes. "But I didn't turn back."

"Why didn't you turn back?"

"Where would I go?"

Bekerman was assigned a job at a pharmacy in Teploye Ozero ("Warm Lake"), a new settlement outside the city, and a room in a barracks to go with the job. Some months after he moved in, a trainload of Jews arrived. "They were all from Odessa," he told me. "They had been evacuated to Siberia, and they weren't allowed to go back. They were rerouted to Birobidzhan."

It seems that the Jews from Ukraine and the Crimea, arriving at the rate of about a thousand families a year starting in 1947, were ones who had tried to return to their homes on the scorched earth of the former Pale only to discover that the native anti-Semitism, reignited by the years of Nazi occupation, was no longer contained by the Soviet authorities. Jews found that they could not reclaim their homes, occupied by non-Jewish locals for years by now, or, often, find jobs or even secure the documents necessary to live legally in their hometowns. The authorities offered an alternative, however: free railroad tickets to Birobidzhan and help reset-tling there.

Birobidzhan authorities were overwhelmed and complained bitterly in reports to party higher-ups: "Local resettlement organizations [in Ukraine] have been acting irresponsibly in selecting settlers for the col-lective farms of our region and, in going after quantity, have sacrificed the most important parameter: quality. Many of the arriving families have no members capable of working. For example, of eighteen families arriving from Belotserkov, twelve had no adult able-bodied family members. We complained about this to the Soviet of Ministers of the USSR [Ukrainian Soviet Socialist Republic] and received an answer acknowledging that our complaints were justified."[7] These were the poor, maimed, weakened, and hungry Jews who no longer had any home anywhere, and they were not welcomed here. Nor did most have anywhere else to go.

More than six hundred families were delivered to Birobidzhan that year, and only forty-one people among the new settlers had any experience working the land. The others—the eighty-one unskilled laborers, forty-three cobblers, thirty-two sales clerks, and the rest—tried to secure jobs in the city and were, for the most part, forcibly removed to the collective farms. A fair number would then be released back to the city for health reasons—tuberculosis was a common diagnosis—while others ran away on their own. As long as they settled in the city of Birobidzhan, the local authorities made little effort to return them to the farms, but warrants were issued for those who fled the region altogether. Without being tried, sentenced, or even accused of a crime—as other ethnic groups exiled by Stalin had been, as the Chechens and the Ingush, for example, had been accused of having cooperated with the German occupiers—the Jews were effectively exiled and tied to this land at the end of the earth.

The land had nothing to offer them. In 1952, a staff member of the resettlement office was sent to investigate settlers' reasons for wanting to leave Birobidzhan. His report was contained in a handwritten note I found in the archives: "They mostly answer not things like the climate or the mosquitoes or illness or it is too far to buy things. Many of them say right out that they have no desire to live here because even if you make enough to have something to eat even then there is no mill on which to grind the grain and so they are forced to eat the kind of bread that is half made up of sand and anyway they would want to see at least one grain mill for each district and there isn't even that."

A 1949 resolution of the Central Committee that called for the resettlement of Jews in Birobidzhan—thereby dashing any hopes anyone still might have held for a Crimean resettlement project—specified that every settler family upon arrival must receive a modest sum of spending money, a housing construction loan, a loan for purchasing a cow, and fifty kilograms of grain per family member, with an additional fifty for the head of household. But grain was in short supply—another epidemic killed the crops of 1949—as were cows. A shipment of goats was promised by another region, but months went by and no livestock arrived; archival documents tell the heartbreakingly tedious story of delegation after delegation being dispatched to secure the goats and returning empty-handed. Instead of dispensing cows, the resettlement authorities issued the families "certificates of cowlessness," which, in some imaginary Birobidzhan, might have entitled them to aid. The housing construction credit was insufficient to finance housing construction, which was one of many reasons—others included lack of building supplies and shortage of skilled labor—that housing construction kept falling further and further behind the plans, which were modest to begin with. In 1949, for example, only 63 houses were constructed, out of 755 that had been planned.

As for Iosif Bekerman, like thousands of others, he had no place left to return to, so he stayed, and he saw the trainload of refugees come in, the ones who had been turned back from Odessa, "and there was this Jewish girl there, oh, she was so beautiful, a real Jewish girl, and I thought, This must be my destiny." He married her and they lived together in Birobidzhan for nearly half a century and had three children together. For decades he dreamed of being able to send for his aunt—the one who had survived the war and had stayed back in Ukraine and who had by now married the only other Jew from their shtetl who had survived—but the Bekerman family only ever had the one room in the barracks, so he never did write to her asking her to come to Birobidzhan.

14

The Black Book would not be published in the Soviet Union. The Ministry of State Security, the MGB (the precursor to the KGB), was filing reports with the Central Committee, recommending that the JAC be shut down. At least one report was signed by Mikhail Suslov, an up-and-coming ideologue who would remain a top Soviet official until his death, in 1982. Suslov's report acknowledged that the JAC had made a positive contribution during the war, but following the Soviet victory the committee's activities were, he wrote, "acquiring an increasingly nationalist, Zionist character and [the JAC] was objectively empowering a Jewish reactionary bourgeois nationalist movement abroad and heating up nationalist Zionist attitudes among some parts of the Jewish population of the USSR."[1]

The Jews were becoming the main enemy within. In January 1948, Mikhoels was reported to have died in a car accident while on a trip to Minsk. Thirty years later, when I was a child, I first heard about Mikhoels from my great-grandmother, who talked about him as a Jewish martyr; she said he was murdered. It was another two decades before the documents were published. She had been right: the legendary Yiddish actor and director was shot dead and left by the side of a highway, for road workers to discover his body in the January snow and to report it as a traffic accident.[2] His funeral in Moscow turned into an unsanctioned public gathering, equal parts outpouring of grief and acknowledgment of dread.

Eynikayt was shut down in November 1948. The Central Committee of the Communist Party ordered the closure of the JAC, which, the decree stated, had become "a center of anti-Soviet propaganda" that "regularly supplies anti-Soviet information to foreign intelligence organizations."[3] Over the course of two weeks, starting on the first anniversary of Mikhoels's murder, everyone in the JAC leadership was arrested; the sixty-four-year-old Bergelson was taken to jail on the last day of the sweep, which means he had been waiting for the arrest for two excruciating and hopeless weeks, with no place left to run. In February, the Politburo took three separate decisions disbanding Jewish writers' associations in Moscow, Kyiv, and Minsk and shutting down Yiddish-language literary journals.[4]

Over the next two years, Bergelson was subjected to several forms of torture. He was beaten; he was occasionally placed in solitary confinement in an unheated six-by-six-foot cell. But more painful than anything else, he was interrogated, often nightly. The interrogations, which would last sleepless night after sleepless night, always ended with the ritual of his reviewing and signing the transcript, which sometimes included some of the things he had actually said—some of them under threat of immediate execution, some of them in a state of hopeless exhaustion, all of them in fear—and many things he'd never said. Occasionally, he found the strength to object. Sometimes he made his own marks on the page.

Once he found the scene comical even while it was taking place. The investigator said that the American Yiddish journalist Ben Zion Goldberg was a spy. "Goldberg was an American spy. Really?" responded Bergelson. It seems to have been the kind of mock-surprised, highly disbelieving "Really?" that in American English is more accurately rendered as "Oh, really?" In Russian, this intonation is marked by double punctuation: "Really?!" At the end of the session, as Bergelson reviewed the transcript, he discovered that his "Really" was followed with a period: "Goldberg was an American spy. Really." Bergelson asked for a correction, but the transcribing secretary said, "We do not have the custom of using double punctuation." Bergelson raised the issue again at trial, months later. It was useless.[5]

The lead investigator in the JAC case was a man named Vladimir Komarov, a state security veteran who would himself be arrested a few years later. He would write the following letter in his own defense:

> Defendants literally trembled before me. They feared me like the plague, feared me more than they did the other investigators. Even the minister [of state security] did not evoke the terror that they showed when I personally interrogated them. Enemies under arrest fully knew and sensed my hatred of them. They saw me as an investigator who had a harsh punitive attitude toward them and therefore, as other investigators told me, they tried in every way to avoid meeting me or having me interrogate them. . . . I especially hated and was merciless toward the Jewish nationalists, whom I saw as the most dangerous and evil enemies. Because of my hatred of them, I was considered an anti-Semite not only by the defendants but by former employees of the MGB who were of Jewish nationality.[6]

Still, the fifteen people under investigation—all of them middle-aged or older, all of them Jews who had seen great sorrow and experienced extreme fear—managed to make the process of fabricating a case against them quite difficult. Two refused to cooperate altogether, signing none of the transcripts and, most important, refusing to libel any of the other defendants. Several people signed their transcripts but recanted in court; they appear to have felt that by signing the transcripts they would ensure that they lived to see the trial. Bergelson was not one of the more difficult defendants, but even his mild-mannered insistence on examining and occasionally correcting the interrogation transcripts was unlike anything most of the Stalinist investigators had ever seen. So it was not until late March 1952, more than three years after the arrests, that the fifteen defendants were given access to the forty-two thick binders that constituted the case against the Jewish Anti-Fascist Committee. They had eight days to read the files and prepare for trial.

The indictment read, in part:

. . . Bergelson's nationalist ideology was formed back in the years of the Civil War, when Bergelson wrote for the reactionary Jewish newspaper *Die neue zeit*, where he published anti-Soviet articles.

As a convinced nationalist, in 1918 Bergelson joined the central committee of the Culture League, an organization that existed on Ukrainian territory, where he carried out work of sabotage against the Soviet state. In 1921, aided by enemies of the people Frumkina and Litvakov (previously sentenced), he deserted the Soviet Union and proceeded to publish anti-Soviet articles in the bourgeois reactionary press for a number of years. In 1934 Bergelson used his enemy connections to return to the Soviet Union, inserted himself into the steering committee of the Jewish section of the Writers Union and continued his enemy activities against the Communist Party.

. . . The investigation has thus established that at the time of the formation of the Jewish Anti-Fascist Committee the accused Bergelson [and twelve other names listed] were enemies of the Soviet regime, ready at any opportunity to increase their work of sabotage against the Party and the Soviet state.

The document went on to say that leaders of the JAC had conspired with American Jews to seize the Crimea and populate it with Jews. In addition, those American Jewish spies had used the JAC to gather information about other parts of the Soviet Union, including Birobidzhan. But worst of all, the JAC had planned to go ahead with the Crimea plan and had even dispatched Kvitko on a reconnaissance trip.

Certain that the Crimea issue would be resolved in their favor and entertaining the illusion that they were now "men of state," Mikhoels, Fefer, Epshteyn, and Bergelson distributed ministerial portfolios among themselves and the most active Jewish nationalists ahead of time.

Every one of the men and women on trial was accused of having met with American Jews in the Soviet Union in order to hand over intelligence information.

> The accused Bergelson in 1945–1946 had repeated meetings in Moscow with [American Jewish activists] Goldberg and Novik, to whom he conveyed some amount of information that interested them about the life of Jews in the USSR and about Birobidzhan.

More insidious than pure fiction, the case contained exhaustive descriptions of things Bergelson actually did, interpreted and presented in a way that doomed him.

> The investigation has established that in addition to their spying, [all of the accused], acting on assignment from reactionary Jewish American circles . . . engaged in broad-based propaganda of bourgeois nationalism among the Jewish population of the USSR. In an attempt to forestall the natural process of assimilation of the Jews and set them up to oppose the Communist Party and the Soviet government, [the accused] used the *Eynikayt* newspaper, Jewish literary journals, the *Der emes* publishing house, [other Yiddish-language media outlets], and the State Jewish Theater to inflame nationalist sentiment among the Jewish population.

On page 231 of volume 18, Bergelson admitted to doing the work to which he had devoted most of his adult life: creating a Jewish cultural hub. He told the investigator,

> "As a result of nationalist work, the Jewish Anti-Fascist Committee was essentially transformed into . . . a nationalist center of the USSR and was able to undertake work to consolidate Jewish nationalist elements and awaken among the Jewish population the desire for nationalist separation. JAC became the sort of place where many Jews came for any reason that may not have had a direct or indirect connection to the committee's work."

The indictment ended with summaries of the defendants' lives and crimes:

David Rafailovich Bergelson, born 1882 in the shtetl of Sarny in Ukraine, of Jewish nationality, descendant from the family of a wealthy trader, a citizen of the USSR, lacking secondary education, a practicing Jewish writer before his arrest, stands accused of engaging in enemy activity against the Communist Party and the Soviet state dating back to the establishment of the Soviet regime. As a member of the presidium of the Jewish Anti-Fascist Committee, he took an active part in collecting information about the Soviet Union on behalf of the Americans, traveled to Kiev with the goal of spying in 1947, and during the visit to the USSR of American intelligence officers Goldberg and Novik handed over information on Birobidzhan, thereby violating articles 58-1a, 58-10 part 2, and 58-11 of the Penal Code.[7]

These Soviet investigators had managed to get Bergelson's birth year and his birthplace wrong, but it was the numbers at the end of the paragraph that mattered. They stood for high treason (punishable by death), seditious propaganda with the use of religious or national prejudice (punishable by death), and conspiracy (punishable by death).[8]

On April 3, 1952, State Security Minister Semyon Ignatyev sent the indictment to Stalin, with a cover letter:

To: Comrade Stalin

I hereby present a copy of the indictment in the case of the Jewish nationalists, American spies Lozovsky, Fefer, and the others. I report that the case has been forwarded for review to the Military Collegium of the Supreme Court of the USSR with the proposal of sentencing Lozovsky, Fefer, and all of their accomplices, with the exception of Shtern, to death by firing squad.

Shtern should be exiled to a distant region for a ten-year term.

S. Ignatyev[9]

Lina Shtern, one of the great natural scientists of the twentieth century, the discoverer of the blood-brain barrier, was a devout Communist and a member of two anti-fascist committees: the Jewish one and the women's one. Executing her might have drawn negative attention in the West. She was one of two women who stood trial alongside Bergelson. The Politburo itself—most likely, Stalin personally—made the final sentencing decisions. It was death by firing squad for all of the defendants except Shtern, who would be sentenced to five years' exile. Only after the sentencing instructions had been conveyed to the MGB could the trial commence. The case was heard by three military judges with neither a prosecutor nor defense attorneys present.[10] Only fourteen exhausted elderly Jews appeared in the courtroom; one was by now too ill to leave his cell. The trial began on May 8, 1952, in secret; records remained classified for four decades afterward.

15

The crackdown in Birobidzhan began within months of Mikhoels's murder. In April 1948 the regional party committee met to discuss the work of *Birobidzhaner shtern*. The newspaper was found to have committed several "mistakes"—there was hardly a more damning word in the Russian language in those days. One of the mistakes was the publication of Emiot's poem "Symphony," which was found to be "lacking any sociopolitical content and entirely divorced from reality." Other sins: 430 of 540 articles examined by a party commission concerned Jews; the newspaper published a list of Jews who had been awarded the Hero of the Soviet Union, the country's highest military honor. For these mistakes, the editor, Buzi Miller, was removed from his post.[1] A year later, he was expelled from the Communist Party "for insincerity and the promotion of bourgeois nationalism."[2]

In July 1949 the Communist Party convened a special two-day conference to discuss the Yiddish nationalist conspiracy. The first secretary of the Khabarovsk regional party committee arrived in Birobidzhan especially for the occasion. This was an unmistakable sign: the leaders of the Jewish Autonomous Region had clearly made such a mess of things that they could no longer be trusted to clean up for themselves. Before the new purges commenced, higher party authorities would have to shine a merciless light on the failings of the Jews. The first secretary, whose name was Yefimov, listed the crimes:

In his novella *Birobidzhan*, the writer Miller postulates that Birobidzhan is the only sole center for Soviet Jews, that only Birobidzhan revived the Jewish people and promised a happy future for those people. . . . After Miller cooked up this anti-Soviet mess, Rabinkov, the Birobidzhan literary critic, praised it as an outstanding piece of creative work, hailing Miller's play *He Is from Birobidzhan*, which is in fact ideologically harmful, and glossing over mistakes of a nationalistic nature found in the poetry of Emiot, thus demonstrating that he himself holds harmful cosmopolitan views. . . . The Jewish poet Lyubov Vasserman, a former Zionist who came to the Soviet Union from Palestine and who to this day holds Zionist nationalist views, was put in charge of literary programming at the regional radio committee and used her position to select for broadcast works of low artistic and conceptual quality but authored by local writers and poets. Nor did she neglect to air her own so-called work, which was seeped in the spirit of nationalism. . . . The work of Birobidzhan writer [Ber] Slutsky also contained mistakes of a nationalistic nature. In his review of *The Birobidzhan Generation*, a book by the Jewish poet Vergelis, Slutsky praised its nationalist assertion that Birobidzhan, and not the Soviet Union, is a homeland for Jews.

Yefimov cited two more examples of "bourgeois nationalism" on the part of Alexander Bakhmutsky, then the head of the Birobidzhan party organization, which made him roughly the equivalent of governor: "He personally took the initiative of organizing an orphanage specifically for Jewish children and then had all the children from this orphanage enrolled in a Jewish school; he also used the regional museum to create a department of Jewish culture, which served as a center of nationalist tendencies." The Birobidzhan leadership accepted aid from an American charitable organization, earmarked, said Yefimov, "for the non-existent Jewish orphans."[3] In other words, Bakhmutsky was simultaneously accused of favoring Jewish orphans and making them up out of thin air.

For two days following this dressing-down, local party leaders, of whom there were many, took the stage in turns, each of them trying to prove not only his own innocence but also someone else's guilt.

"*Birobidzhaner shtern,*" said Mikhail Levitin, chairman of the regional party executive committee, "committed a gross mistake, a bourgeois-nationalist mistake, when it printed a front-page article called 'More Attention Should Be Paid to Propagandizing in the Jewish Language,' asserting that 'the Jewish language is the best and most accessible for the comprehension of Jewish masses' and no mention was made of the great Russian language of Lenin and Stalin."[4]

"Political mistakes enabled bourgeois nationalists, enemies of our motherland like Miller, Rabinkov, Vasserman, and other bastards to do their low deed," contributed Savely Kushnir, secretary of the city party committee.

"Nationalism is currently the biggest danger facing the region," opined regional party committee secretary Zynovy Brokhin. "For example, materials published in the [Russian-language paper] *Birobidzhanskaya zvezda* in May 1944, on the occasion of the tenth anniversary of the Jewish Autonomous Region, compared the heroic feats of Jews in the Great Patriotic War with the biblical story of Samson, they said that 'the lion's heart of the Maccabees beats in their chests.' But how could they make an equal sign between the patriotic feats of the peoples of our country, standing up for the achievements of socialism, and events from Jewish ancient history and biblical tales? Certainly this should not have been allowed!"[5]

"Someone here mentioned a cemetery," said Abram Yarmitsky, deputy chairman of the regional party executive committee, in his own defense, referring to a plan to organize a Jewish burial ground in Birobidzhan. "But there is no Jewish cemetery! We scrapped those plans, because we realized it would have been wrong."[6]

Bakhmutsky, the governor, spoke twice during the conference. On the first day, he tried to walk a fine line between admitting his mistakes and denying his guilt. "It is inarguable," he said, bumbling, "that Vasserman's Zionist moods, Zionist motives in places, and not just in works of literature, if you can call them that, have been known, as have been known the nationalist views of Miller, Rabinkov, Grinberg, and others. . . . This is my big mistake. . . . How can I explain this mistake? How can I explain the fact that I ordered the creation of a Jewish orphanage, or about teaching the Jewish language at the elementary school and essentially creating an artificial Jewish school? The main explanation is that a number of nationalists in the region were doing their work, were popularizing their views in the region and focusing everyone's attention on the fact that Jewish culture here was not developing. I didn't understand the nationalist substance of these views and essentially became beholden to these nationalists."[7]

The following day, Bakhmutsky, disheveled, exhausted, and sleep-deprived, took the stage again, this time solely to beg. He was only thirty-eight years old, he said, and he implored the people in the audience—especially the head of the regional secret police, who sat at the front of the room the entire time—to have mercy. He knew that they would not.

The party conference ended by voting to address a letter to Comrade Stalin, expressing undying gratitude for pointing out the mistakes that had so endangered the region and promising "to cleanse thoroughly our ideological and other institutions of all nationalistic elements as well as all those who cannot be trusted and those who do not work well. . . . We will close the ranks of the Party organization and all those who labor in our region around the Party and the Soviet government, and around you, our dearly beloved Iosif Vissarionovich."[8]

"Cleanse thoroughly" they would. Everyone who had been mentioned during that party conference—including most of the speakers—would be expelled from the party, arrested, and sentenced to years in the labor camps.

16

The regional party committee resolved to shut down *Birobidzhan* in July 1949, "in light of the fact that nationalist elements who have been expelled from the Party were members of its editorial board." A month later, the regional party committee issued a highly classified order to have all copies of *Forpost* and *Birobidzhan* removed from the region's libraries and bookstores. By this time, the members of *Birobidzhan*'s editorial board had been arrested.

In another three months, a series of separate, very precise orders were issued in reference to books by newly identified outlaws, including Emiot, Vasserman, Miller, Bergelson, Fefer, and Markish. "To remove from the libraries and the bookselling network of the Jewish Autonomous Region all copies of the book *Sunrise* by Birobidzhan writer I. Emiot, printed by the Birobidzhan Publishing House in 1948 with a press run of 2 thousand copies and a page count of 62," read one such order. In about a month, the head of the local censorship bureau reported that, fortuitously, 1,930 copies of the book had been removed from the printing plant's warehouse before they ever made it out into the world.[1]

What did they do with all those books? Tens of thousands of volumes, most of them fairly thin, all published on cheap, unevenly colored off-white paper, though those written by Bergelson, as befits a living classic, came in fancy hard covers—the destruction of so many words suddenly turned toxic was no trivial task. The magnitude was huge; the danger was palpable. There was no place safe enough and large enough to intern so many books; there was no local facility capable of pulping them. So the

Birobidzhan authorities did the only logical thing. Five years after the end of the Second World War, the Sholem Aleichem Library of the Jewish Autonomous Region staged a book burning (or two, according to some sources) in its courtyard, to destroy every Yiddish-language book that had been found in the region.[2]

A policy of Russification was applied to Birobidzhan much as it had been to places like Chechnya, from which the indigenous Muslim population had been deported by Stalin. The orphanage was methodically Russified. First, preschool-aged children were transferred to a different home, separated from their older siblings and their Jewish identity at the same time. Then Yiddish was abolished as the primary language of instruction at School Number Two, which the orphans had been attending; from now on all subjects would be taught in Russian. Finally, a group of medics convened at the orphanage to conduct a particular sort of inspection, the sort to which the children's dead fathers and older brothers had been subjected by the Nazis: boys fourteen and over were divided into two groups, depending on whether they were circumcised. Those who could pass would be shipped off to trade schools all over the Far East, where, in addition to low-level skills, they would most often acquire new identity documents and new, non-Jewish names. With the population of the orphanage thus reduced, ethnic Russian children were shipped into Birobidzhan to take the vacant spots and help eradicate the institution's Jewish identity.

Come vacation time, though, many of the Jewish kids attending trade schools hundreds of miles away showed up at their native orphanage, often having traveled on the roofs of train cars. Anna Kogan, the kindly Jewish woman who was now running the home, would welcome these kids for the weeks of their vacation and even find the money to get them tickets back to their trade schools. "When I was living in Birobidzhan in the 1960s, I would occasionally run into other former kids from the orphanage," recalled one of the few who maintained a Jewish identity in trade-school exile. "Izya Temnorod would always ask me, 'Where is my brother, who was sent to the same trade school as you?' I didn't have the heart to tell him that his brother, Motya, changed his name to Dmitry and his ethnicity to Ukrainian, moved to the [central Russian] city of Penza and wanted to have nothing to do with his own brother."[3]

The Jews of Birobidzhan stopped speaking Yiddish. No one had declared it lingua non grata, as had been done with Hebrew decades earlier, but with Yiddish schools switching to Russian and Yiddish writers being dressed down publicly, Yiddish itself no longer dared speak its name. People purposefully switched to using Russian as their everyday language, not only in open places and on public transportation but even at home, for there was still no privacy anywhere in Birobidzhan—with dozens of families sharing kitchens, bathrooms, and hallways, a careless word was liable to be overheard. The fear extended to reading in Yiddish, too. The number of subscribers to *Birobidzhaner shtern* went from an (admittedly unimpressive) average of 610 in 1947 to 134 in 1950[4]—a precipitous drop that, especially in light of the continued growth of Birobidzhan's Jewish population, could only be explained by fear.

It was no longer an oasis free of anti-Semitism. Iosif Bekerman, the pharmacist who had dreamed of Birobidzhan after losing his entire family in Ukraine, had barely started at his job at Teploye Ozero, a settlement outside the city of Birobidzhan, when he noticed "people looking at me funny, you know, because I am a Jew running a pharmacy. Then people stopped saying hello to me. Like I was guilty of something. And then they sent in a lecturer, they gathered all of us together, and he told us about the cosmopolitans, the Jewish cosmopolitans, he said they were so bad." "Rootless cosmopolitans" were the official targets of Stalin's anti-Semitic campaign; the term implied that these were people devoid of clear loyalties, people not to be trusted. "I wanted to say to them," Bekerman told me about those who had begun to shun him, "that even if the people they were talking about—even if they made mistakes, why do they necessarily need to be arrested, why do they need to be executed? Why can't you just have talks with them, do the work, you know, clarify the issues for them? But someone told me, If you stand up for them, you'll be joining them. This was how it was, so we were all silent. We knew a lot, but we were silent. We were each afraid for ourselves, and none of us could do anything."[5]

Seven writers who had worked to popularize Birobidzhan for postwar settlers now stood accused of organizing a secret nationalist organization. Itsik Fefer, in pretrial detention in Moscow and testifying against his fellow JAC leaders, testified against these writers, too: he gave a statement condemning them as nationalists. Among the writers was Buzi Miller, the deposed editor of *Birobidzhaner shtern*. The investigator demanded that he explain why the newspaper had published a list of Jewish war heroes.

"Why is the list titled 'Honor and Glory to the Jewish People'? Are you unaware that this definition—*the Jewish people*—contradicts the nationalities policy of the Party and the government?"[6]

At first Miller insisted that he had made "no nationalistic mistakes," but after three months of interrogations and torture by sleeplessness, he caved.

> INTERROGATOR: The newspaper *Birobidzhaner shtern*, which you edited, frequently used the term "Jewish statehood." There were very few articles devoted to the indestructible friendship of the peoples. Did you consciously publish such articles?
> MILLER: Yes, it was conscious.
> INTERROGATOR: So this was a consequence of your nationalistic views?
> MILLER: Yes, I held nationalistic views.[7]

Lyubov Vasserman was confronted with the manuscript of a poem.

> INTERROGATOR: Here is another poem that was confiscated during the search of your apartment. Did you write this?
> VASSERMAN: Yes, the poem I am currently being shown was found in my apartment during the search. I wrote it in 1947.
> INTERROGATOR: Do you admit that it is a nationalist poem?
> VASSERMAN: Yes, because it contains a nationalistic expression: "I love Birobidzhan, my country."

INTERROGATOR: So you admit that you consciously propagated nationalism.

VASSERMAN: No, I do not. Because I never published this poem and no one ever read it. When I wrote the poem, I immediately realized that it was nationalistic.[8]

In the case of the Birobidzhan writers, there was no pretense of a trial. They were simply handed their sentences at the end of the interrogation process: ten years of hard labor.

17

In a Soviet court—and, now, in Russian courts—pleas are entered after the initial set of motions, which is how it happened that Bergelson addressed his fiction first and his life second. On the first day of the trial, he petitioned to have some of his writing included in the case, "because the indictment says that while I was living abroad I was always writing against the Soviet Union, but if you read my collection of short stories, you will see that I did not always write against the Soviet Union, I only did it for a time."[1]

Five people, including Markish and Solomon Lozovsky, the propaganda executive who had helped form the JAC, pleaded not guilty. Two pleaded guilty. Seven, including Kvitko, Hofshteyn, and Bergelson, pleaded "guilty in part."[2]

The trial began with testimony by Fefer, a poet Bergelson had known for more than thirty years. He had accompanied Mikhoels to America during the fund-raising trip in 1943—it was understood then that he was a secret police agent, placed by Mikhoels's side to keep an eye on him. Now he was on trial, but he was also a cooperating witness; he had been promised leniency. He had entered a plea of guilty. He took the stand to begin building the case against the others, reaching back to 1920 to do so. "Nationalist attitudes are in essence anti-Soviet attitudes," he said. "Bergelson and Hofshteyn expressed their nationalist attitudes in their literary work." The work of *Eynikayt* during the war similarly engaged in nationalist propaganda by singling out Jewish war heroes as well as Jewish victims of Nazism, he claimed. The height of anti-Soviet nationalism, Fefer testified, was reached when the committee activists picked up the Crimea idea, which had been proposed by the Americans.[3]

Markish, who had lived a life almost perfectly parallel to Bergelson's, was interrogated on the third day of the trial. The two had never liked each other, and now Markish told the judges as much. Unlike Bergelson, he pleaded not guilty, but he answered the judges' questions in detail, with what might even have seemed to be eagerness; like perhaps a majority of defendants in Stalinist courts, he fully recognized the court's authority and saw the case against him not as a willful mangling of reality but as a discrete, unfortunate misunderstanding that could be corrected. He testified about the American journalist Ben Zion Goldberg's extended stay in the Soviet Union in 1946; back then it had seemed like a breakthrough for the Soviet Union, a prominent journalist staying in the country for six months, filing extraordinarily pro-Soviet reports,[4] but now he was supposed to have been the defendants' American spymaster.

"He asked me, 'Why didn't the Birobidzhan initiative succeed?'" Markish testified about Goldberg. "And I said, 'What Jew would trade Moscow for Birobidzhan?'"

"So you told him of your anti-Birobidzhan convictions?" the presiding judge asked.

"I was in Birobidzhan in 1934, when I was writing a book on the border patrol. I remembered Birobidzhan not as a place but as people who were living on the border. . . . What was my attitude toward Birobidzhan in 1934? I thought it was a place for Jews who wanted to work the land, or to be fishermen. . . . I didn't believe that an intelligent Jew might choose to live in Birobidzhan when he had everything here. People who have the mentality of flies, people who need to show themselves off to seem bigger, they need those kinds of places to stand on."[5]

Was Birobidzhan on trial? No, but Bergelson was. And Markish, who had known him since both were in their twenties, now acted as though the espionage charges were not entirely fantastical. Or, even more absurdly, he thought he might be able to play his own game against Fefer, the informant. Testifying two days later, he articulated his vision of how each member of the JAC had participated in the espionage:

MARKISH: Bergelson was the most avid supporter of the Jewish national cultural tradition of anybody on the committee. They all respected him. He is an old writer, he is known in America, he writes about the traditions of the old world, so he represented the kind of culture the Anti-Fascist Committee needed.

PRESIDING JUDGE: He was an appropriate person for the sort of criminal activity the committee later led?

MARKISH: I could only say that about the committee's nationalist activities. I have thought about whether I agree that they were spies. I can believe that of Fefer, but I can't imagine that Bergelson was a spy.[6]

This was perhaps the strangest thing about the trial, this warped reality in which one made fine distinctions between fantastical charges of espionage and cultural activism, which had miraculously been transformed into a crime called "nationalist activity." In the absence of defense attorneys, in the absence even of prosecutors, with the knowledge that sentences had been passed long before the trial began, fourteen old Jews spent entire days telling their life stories, pointing fingers at people they had known their whole lives, expounding on the finer points of absurdity—and believing that it mattered. Bergelson was no exception.

Markish's testimony lasted almost three days. Bergelson's commenced a few minutes after Markish finished, just past nine in the evening on May 13, 1952. "I was brought up in the spirit of nationalism," he began. "I saw no other spirit anywhere around me until the age of seventeen. There was not a single book in Russian around when I was a child."

It began as a confession. "There is a day in August," Bergelson said, "when the temple of Solomon burned down. On this day all Jews, even the children, fast for a twenty-four-hour period. They go to the cemetery for the entire day to pray 'among the dead,' and I was so seeped in the atmosphere of the burning of the temple, people talked so much about this, that when I was six or seven years old, I felt I could sense the smell of the smoke and the fire. I tell you this to show how deep-seated the nationalism was."

He told the court of his mother's death, and of living with his older brothers and having to pay for his keep. He told the three military judges, whose primary job was signing pre-scripted death verdicts, of starting to write, of struggling to break onto the literary scene, and of the recognition he received much later, when his best novel was published in Russian in 1939. He then blamed his old rival Moyshe Litvakov, executed on a terrorism conviction more than a decade ago, for trying to turn Bergelson into a Territorialist.

"What was their goal?" the presiding judge asked about the Territorialists.

"To procure a territory for the Jews. Gradually, he began to influence me a bit, in the nationalist way."

Bergelson did not mention that back when Litvakov was arrested, he'd signed a letter condemning his activities, as one did if one wished to survive. He perhaps hoped that the court knew about the letter.

He told the court about living in Kyiv after the Bolshevik revolution. "The regimes changed frequently. Before 1921, there were many regimes: there were Denikin, the Germans, Petlyura," he said, listing the names of some of the Soviet regime's most villainized enemies. He seemed to be damning himself by placing himself in this context and at the same time making a hopeless play for human sympathy. "It was the kind of time when a person who has nationalism in his blood can't get his bearings, he can't tell where he is or who he is with." He called the Kultur-Lige, that heady attempt at bringing to life an autonomous Yiddish world, a nationalist organization—nationalist not, clearly, in the Dubnowian sense of promoting cultural cohesion but nationalist in the Soviet sense of pure anti-Bolshevik evil.

"I didn't believe the Bolsheviks would win," he said. Today this, too, may sound like a play for sympathy, but in 1952 this confession of lack of faith was pure self-flagellation. "I had no hatred for the Bolsheviks," he said. "I even liked them because, in a way, they had saved my life. But my nationalist friends told me this was all ephemeral and would pass. This was my attitude toward the Bolsheviks." He said he had worked for a newspaper, and he then appealed to other defendants to testify as to the content of the articles he had written thirty-five years earlier. He said it was not all nationalist.

The court, however, had no tolerance for the defendants' attempts to clear their names in any way. The presiding judge demanded that Bergelson continue the self-flagellation: "You stand accused of having opposed the October Revolution. . . . You must testify as to the substance of the charges. Tell the court how you opposed the Soviet regime."

Bergelson seemed to search his memory for further evidence he could provide against himself. "It seems to me that opposition has to take the form of some sort of action. So what were my actions?" he asked himself on the stand. "My opposition to the Soviet Union took the form that I fled the Soviet Union." The man who had spent half his life running to save his life and had then paid what he thought were all his dues for the right to return to the Soviet Union was now suggesting his very emigration could be seen as treason.

The presiding judge wanted Bergelson to drive this point home. "Let's finish with this period of your life," he said. "Why you fled. The Soviet system had saved you. . . . This was your response to your own salvation, to the salvation of the Jews. The attitudes toward Jews had changed drastically, pogroms had ceased, Jews were granted equal rights—why under these conditions did you need to flee the country?"

The judge's list of the Bolsheviks' gifts to the Jews was factually accurate. Bergelson had said as much himself. But now the court was demanding that he describe how his most basic instincts worked, that he articulate the finely tuned sense of impending doom that had caused him to run. Bergelson explained that things had been very difficult in Kyiv. That was the winter he had written the desperate appeal to American Jews on behalf of the Yiddish writers of Kyiv. He now said he regretted writing the letter. He said he came to Moscow in 1920 and felt at loose ends. "I felt I should be writing, but I couldn't write, it seemed I could do nothing, it seemed I had no talent, and we were hungry, and it was hard." An invitation to go to Berlin and be published proved too tempting to reject. Bergelson began to describe the circuitous route he took to Berlin, then caught himself trying to justify his treason. "It is now that I consider my fleeing the Soviet Union to be an enemy act," he explained. "Back then, I did not see it that way."

Bergelson spent all day testifying about his treason through emigration.

18

The following day, Bergelson testified about Birobidzhan and OZET, the Committee for the Settlement of Toiling Jews on the Land. The prosecution's case classified OZET's work as enemy activity.

"So you were worried about assimilation?" asked the presiding judge.

"It's not that I didn't believe in assimilation," Bergelson said vaguely. "It's that I thought it could be a very long process. And that would mean a prolonged agony, which can be worse than death."

"Do you still believe assimilation of the Jews among the Soviet people to be akin to agony?"

"I'm not speaking of the people; I am speaking of the culture."

"Where there is culture, there is the people?"

"I was so steeped in the ideas of the Soviet Union, I could actually be happy in the end, knowing that the Jewish people were living among other peoples."

Something had changed overnight: Bergelson was now trying to deflect some of the accusations, if not deny them outright. So the presiding judge asked a question that could not be deflected: he demanded to know what exactly was discussed "during the anti-Soviet gatherings at your apartment." Bergelson struggled to deny the premise of the question, and failed.

"So you didn't hold special gatherings, but as soon as you got together, the talk would begin?" the judge pressed.

"Yes, that's correct," admitted Bergelson.

"Answer specifically," the presiding judge instructed. "Did the Jewish Section of the Union of Soviet Writers dispatch its allies to other cities, where lectures and other events devoted to nationalist themes were conducted?"

"The section did dispatch its members, yes. There were events held, there were themes that, in essence, were nationalist. Their goal was the desire to broaden Jewish culture, to make it flower, to have it engage the masses."

"The lectures and the talks were in the Jewish language?"

"Yes, in the Jewish language."

"So what is there to deny?" the judge demanded.

This lasted all day, and continued the next, May 15.

"So does this mean that the Jewish Anti-Fascist Committee, in both oral and written propaganda, engaged in the glorification of Biblical images and preached the unity of the Jews of the entire world based solely on their having common blood, with no regard for class distinctions?"

"The glorification of Biblical images would slip in everywhere," admitted Bergelson. "It happened in work, in conversation, and in poems. I don't see what's criminal about this. There are images that it is very appropriate to glorify. It can happen that the glorification of certain images yields some very useful ideas." In the face of death, the nonbelieving son of a pious Jew chose to try to defend this one thing: the images from the holy book of his childhood. Perhaps he was thinking of that day, in August 1941, when he had used the words from a Hebrew psalm, "I shall not die, but live," and they heralded a period of several years when he believed every word he wrote.

The presiding judge was thinking of the very same period of time. He picked up a piece of paper and read out loud, his voice brimming with disdain: it was Bergelson's open letter to the Jews of the world. "This appeal calls on every Jew to take the oath 'I am a child of the Jewish people' and so on. This is a call to unity on the basis of common blood, isn't it?"

"The appeal discusses unity in the fight against fascism."

"So you think Jews are the only people fighting fascism?"

The official Soviet historiography of the Second World War had by now taken hold. The war had been fought by the anti-fascists against the fascists. Any special role of the Jews, including their role as victims, was interpreted as an effort to undermine this narrative. The only special roles belonged to Soviet soldiers, as fighters against fascism, and Communists, as its victims. This, too, made the publication of *The Black Book* impossible.

Bergelson was also accused of libeling the Soviet Union by claiming that anti-Semitism was rampant in postwar Ukraine. He had been wise enough not to write about this issue, and to stay out of the entire postwar Crimea effort, but a witness had apparently testified that "Bergelson, upon learning that the most pronounced desire to move to the Jewish Autonomous Region was observed among Jews residing in Ukraine, told me, libelously, that he had information that anti-Semitism was growing in Ukraine and that the situation there was already quite tense. Continuing this conversation, Bergelson spoke about himself and said that he wanted to go to the Jewish Autonomous Region, where, as he said, 'I could die.'"

"That last sentence is true," said Bergelson. "I said that I wanted to move to Birobidzhan and live there."

Bergelson had entered a plea of "guilty in part." The presiding judge now asked him to which of the charges he was pleading guilty.

"I am guilty of nationalism," he said, "and I am guilty of fleeing the Soviet Union."[1]

He finished testifying on May 15. On July 18, thirteen old Jews were sentenced to death by firing squad. A fourteenth defendant, the one who had been too ill to stand trial, was dying in prison. The fifteenth, Lina Shtern, was sentenced to five years' exile, as per the Kremlin's instructions. They had lied to Fefer, the secret-police agent: for all his cooperation, he would now be shot, too, alongside the people he had helped set up. On August 12, 1952, Bergelson's sixty-eighth birthday, he was executed.[2] For decades, before the transcripts of the trial became accessible to the public following the collapse of the Soviet Union, the date was known, and observed in many Jewish communities the world over, as the Night of the Murdered Poets. There was no accurate information about the number of victims of the execution, or their precise identities, but somehow word got out that there were poets. Markish, Kvitko, Hofshteyn, and Fefer had indeed been poets. Other defendants included journalists, a doctor, a scientist, a scholar, a theater director, and the writer Bergelson, who had gone to his death doing what he had always done: trying to square the circle of Jewishness in a world that did not want Jews, protecting the seeds of a religion he did not practice, and insisting on his right to try to keep alive a dying language.

The JAC trial was to launch a new chapter of Stalinist terror. In addition to the defendants in Moscow, 110 people had been arrested and sentenced to hard labor or death in connection with the JAC. Other Yiddishists had been rounded up and sentenced without a trial; Der Nister had died in a prison hospital in 1950. Next would come the trial of the Jewish doctors, who were accused of poisoning Central Committee members under the guise of treating them. They would be sentenced to death. That would unleash a wave of anti-Semitism so strong that the government would have to deport all Soviet Jews to Birobidzhan for their own protection. Or such were the rumors in Moscow, so frightening and so vivid that my grandmother could recount them to me in great detail decades later.

The doctors were arrested within a few months of the JAC execution. But on March 5, 1953, Stalin died. A month later, the charges against the doctors were dropped, and they were released. The misnamed Night of the Murdered Poets would go down in history as Stalin's last execution. Two years later, the Military Collegium of the Supreme Court of the Soviet Union reviewed the case and acquitted all the defendants, only one of whom, Lina Shtern, was still alive.[3]

19

The jailed Yiddish writers of Birobidzhan had to wait two to three years after Stalin's death for their release—and even then they were amnestied, not cleared of charges. The oldest of them, seventy-two at the time of sentencing, died in prison. The rest returned, at least for a time, to Birobidzhan. It had become just another Far Eastern province—different, and remarkable, in name only. The *New York Times*' Harrison Salisbury, the only foreign correspondent to have diligently covered rumors of the impending Jewish deportation (his stories were never published, but my own grandmother, who censored American correspondents' dispatches, remembered them for decades), hastened to Birobidzhan as soon as he was able to secure permission to travel there, in 1954. "It was plain that Birobidzhan had lost its significance as a Jewish center a long time ago," he reported. "I could not see that the place had any special Jewish character."[1]

The library, however, still bore Sholem Aleichem's name. Soon after returning from prison, the Yiddish writers gathered there for a reading. The room filled to capacity. "The representative of the Department of Culture and Education, speaking Russian, was interrupted continuously by shouts of 'Yiddish! Yiddish!'" recalled Emiot in his memoir, written in the 1970s in Rochester, New York, where he lived for the last twenty years of his life.

There is a picture in the collection of the Birobidzhan museum: six triumphant-looking Yiddish writers, four of whom had spent seven years in the camps, holding up a copy of a journal in which all of them were once again published. Lyubov Vasserman, sitting in the middle, is beaming, as though justice could indeed be restored, as though a Yiddish writer could claim a motherland in the Soviet Union.

She stayed in Birobidzhan because she believed in it. She had a brother, a trade-union organizer, who lived in Israel and tried to persuade her to join him there. She would not budge; she said that she had been a "no one" in Palestine, where she had worked as a domestic, and she was someone in Birobidzhan, a Jewish writer. Her brother reportedly pointed out that she was "someone" only in the context and the company of the ten other Jewish writers in Birobidzhan, but this clearly did not work. Long after she was widowed and only after she had become so frail that she could no longer care for herself did Vasserman agree to be moved to Kishinev, Moldova, where her son lived. She spent the last three years of her life in the city of the great pogrom of 1903. She left a book of poetry, published posthumously, called *Birobidzhan, My Home.* As was her wish, these same words are inscribed on her tombstone in the Kishinev cemetery—over the drawing of an open book designed by her son.[2]

Little remains of the post-Stalin history of Birobidzhan, aside from Vasserman's exalted account and Salisbury's bemused one. In 1956, the Israeli ambassador to Moscow, Yosef Avidar, and his wife, Yemima Tchernovitz-Avidar, a popular Israeli children's author, managed to organize an unofficial two-day trip to the Jewish Autonomous Region. They then succeeded in breaking away, briefly, from their handlers, who had concocted a Jewish Potemkin tour. They went back to their hotel room around four in the afternoon on Saturday, the second day of their visit. Presently a woman showed up at their door. "She started asking us questions about Israel," Yemima Tchernovitz-Avidar wrote in her journal. "She was mostly interested in the culture. . . . She turned out to be knowledgeable about the [Hebrew] language and literature. . . . She did not attempt to put a gloss on her life there. 'I have no close friends here or anyone who understands me. I gave my daughter the Hebrew name Shushana, for I myself have a Hebrew name, Hemda bat Shmuel, but what does she know of Jewishness? She remembers the Hebrew lullabies I sang for her, like "Sham shualim yesh," but now she goes by the name Susanna, is married to a Russian man, had adopted a non-Jewish child. . . . But my heart aches for the Jewish word.' . . . She asked for a book in Hebrew, asked if she could read my stories. I said, 'If I send it to you from Moscow, will you come to the post office to pick it up?' She said, 'Send me the Tanakh. Send me anything. I am not afraid. You can send it right to my home address.' She opened the Tanakh and began to read the Song of Songs in a voice as rusty as a door that has been forced open after many years."

A short while later, there was another knock on the door: another aging Hebrew speaker wanted to see the Israelis. "When the old man saw the Tanakh in Hemda's hands, tears came to his eyes. He took the book in his hands and would not let go. 'I burned a large library during the purges, but when I was about to burn the books of Bialik, I said, Enough! Let the fate of this book be my fate! If I survive, so will the book, but if I die, let it be taken from me. So I remain now with a book of Bialik poems, and nothing else.' There we sat, the four of us, these two representatives of a Hebrew world that had been entirely destroyed here and the two of us, who had so much to offer them. We were like two people carrying full jugs of water meeting two others who had been lost in the desert, dying of thirst. . . . I think it was the old man who first started singing [the Tchernichovsky ballad] 'Sakhi, sakhi al halomot' (Laugh, laugh at me, laugh at my dreams). Hemda picked up and then we did. When [the handler] Dukhno came in and saw the four of us singing, he was flabbergasted. He sat down with us, but he was too ignorant to understand anything: he was a worthy student of *Birobidzhaner shtern*." The Avidars found their Birobidzhan encounters so upsetting that they cut their visit short, taking the train on Saturday night rather than Sunday.

20

In the fall of 2009, I traveled to Birobidzhan. Contrary to my expectations and my experience of the Russian Far East, I found Birobidzhan pretty in places. It has ambition, which is evident in the width and length of its avenues and the amount of stone that was used to build a new embankment to mark the seventy-fifth anniversary of the Jewish Autonomous Region. The embankment, with a long promenade, an elaborate balustrade, and a series of statues and decorative benches, is, like so much of Birobidzhan, an unconscious exercise in the falsification of history. There is a gazebo and, next to it, the statue of a seated man in a top hat—as though someone might have been transplanted here from a warmer climate as long as two hundred years ago and spent time by the side of the river. In fact, as we know, the first Europeans got here quite a bit later—and when they did, the river valley was swampland.

An eight-hour flight from Moscow, with a two-hour train ride on top, Birobidzhan is an unlikely destination for tourists—the last time it saw an influx of foreigners was in the late 1980s and early 1990s, when the Soviet authorities lifted the travel ban on foreigners journeying into the border zones and correspondents rushed to see the tantalizingly named Jewish Autonomous Region. But it has a decent tourist infrastructure, all of it geared to the Jewish curiosity seeker. There are two main avenues, one named for Sholem Aleichem and the other for Lenin; the former has a pedestrian-only zone and the latter boasts a series of memorial plaques. The Sholem Aleichem Library, the regional museum, the synagogue, and the Jewish community center are all located along Lenin Street, as are two newly constructed Russian Orthodox churches. The memorial boards are in three languages: Russian, English, and Yiddish. Iosif Bekerman, the one surviving settler, once complained to the library authorities that the Yiddish text contained a mistake: it claimed that Lyubov Vasserman and other Yiddish notables had worked at the library "in Sholem Aleichem's lifetime." (The great Yiddish writer died a dozen years before the first Jewish settler arrived in Birobidzhan.) "They told me it doesn't matter since no one can read it anyway," Bekerman said to me, still evidently hurt.

As the last of the Yiddish-speaking Jews die, their descendants occasionally find Yiddish-language books in hidden storage spaces in their homes, the heroic feat of having once concealed these banned books rendered obscure by the passage of time and the death of the language. They usually donate the volumes to the Sholem Aleichem Library, which has so little use for them that it recently sent a portion to the local museum of Valdheym, one of the first Jewish collective farms, located just outside of the city. There, the books are displayed under glass. "No one can read them anyway," the keeper explained to me.

The museum keeper's name was Maria Rak. She had been brought to Birobidzhan as a baby, a couple of years before the Second World War, lost both parents early—her father was killed in the war, her mother died when Maria was nine—and was raised by her grandparents in postwar Birobidzhan. Left largely to her own devices, she spent most of her time at school, learning to be a good Komsomol leader. For her outstanding leadership qualities, at the age of seventeen, as soon as she finished school, she was chosen to set up a library at a new settlement.

"They were sent here from Ukraine," she said of the then-new arrivals.

"Jews?" I asked.

"No," she said matter-of-factly. "Nazi collaborators. They were exiled here."

Someone must have thought it either hilarious or brilliant to exile Ukrainian Nazi collaborators to suffer among the Jews in their autonomous region. Birobidzhan is full of comical mismatches, most of them less sinister than this. There is the synagogue—and the Jewish community center, unironically named Freud (*joy* in Yiddish)—on Lenin Street. There is the largest building in Birobidzhan, an angular seventies-style concrete structure on the embankment. It is called the Birobidzhan Philharmonic, and it was constructed to house the Jewish Chamber Theater, which was actually a Moscow troupe that never spent more than a few weeks at a time in its official home city but had an extraordinarily enterprising founder who essentially managed to swindle the construction of the building out of local party bosses. Then there is the question of Jewish food. Valery Gurevich, a deputy governor unofficially in charge of Jewish culture, directed me to the Chinese restaurant at the Philharmonic; he claimed the proprietor, a Chinese man who went by the Russian name of Kolya, had learned the art of Jewish cooking from his Jewish grandmother. But the waiters at the restaurant told me that the Jewish part of the menu had been abolished for lack of demand. In my continuing quest for Jewish food, the following evening I ended up at Café California, ordering a *schnitzel à la Birobidzhan;* it turned out to be made of pork. On the third night, I scored some gefilte fish at the restaurant at my hotel; this dish, which is usually served cold or at room temperature, had been taken out of a jar and *reheated.*

There is the region's flag, adopted around the time of the collapse of the Soviet Union; it is a seven-colored rainbow. The Birobidzhan museum's deputy director giggled when she told me about it—in the intervening twenty years, information that the internationally known gay-pride flag also features a rainbow had reached Birobidzhan. She could not explain why the rainbow had been chosen to represent the region. In 2015, as Russia ramped up its anti-gay campaign, the flag was examined for evidence of homosexual propaganda, and cleared.

I liked the museum. I have been to dozens of these small regional museums in the former Soviet Union, and I fancy myself something of a specialist in their many ways of misapprehending history. All local Russian museums begin with rocks. They are the ideal museum exhibit: rocks do not need to be rearranged in case of a regime shift. In the Birobidzhan museum, rocks take up the entire first floor. Upstairs, I found three rooms devoted to the history of the Jewish Autonomous Region—one each for the prewar, war, and postwar years.

The prewar room begins with an exhibit whose own history I was able gradually to reconstruct. In the late 1980s, the staff of the museum apparently wanted to put the *Jewish* back into the museum of the autonomous region, but all evidence of Jewishness had been destroyed. So they organized an expedition to what had been a shtetl in what had been the Pale of Settlement. As a result, a visitor to the second floor of the Birobidzhan Regional Museum is greeted by the picture of an old, bent Jew with tefillin and a prayer shawl, captioned, "There is only one person left in this old shtetl who remembers how to put on traditional clothing"; a picture of the old shtetl synagogue, now a canning factory; and a glass display case with the "everyday objects of Jewish life," which include a stringless fiddle. The rest of the room covers the earliest stage of Birobidzhan history, from the arrival of the first settlers and the establishment of the autonomous region to a detailed account of the purges of the late 1930s.

The next room, like most war rooms in most Russian museums, has no identity of its own; it is the canned canon of the Great Patriotic War, reproduced faithfully in every regional, school, and workplace museum all over the country. The room is draped in red flags, and it drips Soviet patriotism. Many such war rooms in other museums are dedicated to the heroism of Alexander Matrosov, a nineteen-year-old soldier who threw himself on the opening of a German bunker, thus shielding his comrades from fire. This feat of turning oneself literally into cannon fodder has long been the Soviet definition of heroism.

Birobidzhan, as it happened, had its own hero of similar standing, Iosif Bumagin. Born in Vitebsk in 1907, he joined the Red Army in 1929 and served for four years. He moved to Birobidzhan in 1937 and worked at the one big industrial plant in town. He was drafted again in May 1941, before the German invasion. Purges had decimated the Red Army, and Bumagin was among those chosen for officer training; his credentials were seven years of formal schooling, four years of military service, and years of working as a Communist organizer. He managed to stay at military school virtually until the end of the war, joining the front in April 1945, in Germany. It was during the storming of Breslau, just two weeks before the war in Europe ended, that Bumagin used his own body to silence a German machine gun.[1] The Birobidzhan Museum did not tell me any of this; rather, the exhibit informs the visitor that "Iosif Bumagin repeated the feat of Alexander Matrosov," and for this an entire neighborhood of Birobidzhan is named after him. That is the only local color in the war room, which, oddly, does not even make any mention of the Japanese front, which was virtually a stone's throw from here.

The third and final room has the most difficult job. Whoever put together the first display cases clearly could not make up his mind whether they were devoted to the Yiddish literature and culture of Birobidzhan or to the purges of the late 1940s. As a result, both stories are mangled, a collection of stand-alone pictures—David Bergelson, Lyubov Vasserman, the Jewish theater, a copy of another local writer's book—with brief captions that do not add up to stories:

"D. R. Bergelson. The first leader of a writing group in Birobidzhan in the 1930s. Arrested, executed in 1952."

"Poet I. B. Keller. Arrested in 1948. While incarcerated, wrote and concealed 80 poems. Released in 1956."

It gets even more confusing after that. A couple of displays show sterile, unidentifiable pictures of the Soviet Union in the era of stagnation, a period when Birobidzhan seemed no longer Jewish and the entire country had reached almost total uniformity, with identical people wearing identical clothes living in identical buildings working identical jobs. Skip over perestroika and the collapse of the Soviet Union—a few uncaptioned pictures of Yeltsin and public rallies gloss over the fact that most of Birobidzhan's Jews emigrated to Israel during this period—to end with present-day Birobidzhan, which holds biannual Jewish culture festivals but balances them with Slavic culture festivals in the off-years.

I visited the museum on a day in early October, when the sun outside was still bright enough to let me walk around wearing a light coat but it was already brutally cold in this unheated building, where I made a detailed inventory of the displays. I left the building with an uneasy feeling, the sense of something missing. Something big. Something essential. Something catastrophic.

It took me another few hours to realize that I had just spent an entire day at a Jewish museum that made no mention of the Holocaust. It was as if the Jews of the shtetlach from that first display case had just vanished, disappeared into history for no apparent reason. It was as though there had been no reason for the new influx of Jews after the war. It was as though history, and Birobidzhan itself, had just happened.

That view of history is the post-Soviet condition. What happened to people—to families that still carry the memory, whose physical and psychic scars are plainly visible—was so enormous and so inexplicable, and, worst of all, the victims and their executioners were so intimately entangled, so indistinguishable at times, that, following a brief and torturous period of examination, the country's population has conspired to treat it as a force of nature. I went to the Birobidzhan State Archives, a fortress-like concrete building where local government and party documents are maintained. I was allowed to read most of the documents that concerned settlers and settlement, but when I asked for files from the 1949 party conference that launched the Birobidzhan purges, the young librarian on duty blanched, blushed, then blanched again.

"I'm afraid we cannot give you that file," she said.

"Why not?"

"It's a personnel file. It contains confidential information."

I tried to explain to her that dead people have no right to confidentiality, that the file itself concerned official proceedings and could not be considered confidential, but I did not even broach the topic of how the story of Stalin's purges needed to be told, and told again, if the country were to have any chance of reclaiming its history and moving beyond it. Visibly embarrassed and even scared, the librarian refused to budge.

"People might be disturbed," she explained.

That was the argument used all over Russia in the early 1990s, when, after a year or two during which access to KGB and party archives was truly open, the authorities began the process of restricting it. If I had waited another few years to visit Birobidzhan, I suspect, I would not even have found the documents in the catalog. Eventually, I dug up a locally published volume by a local historian, David Vayserman, who had gained access to the files in more liberal times and faithfully copied them down.

Another artifact of those days, about twenty years earlier, when the post-Soviet citizenry was briefly engaged with its history was the permanent glassed-in display in the archives' on-site museum. It contained copies of some of the documents to which I had been denied access—but the case was sealed shut, so I still could not touch them or read them in their entirety.

"In 1949–1953 a full-fledged cleansing of the state and Party apparatus began all over the country," the anonymous curator informed me through captions. "A campaign against so-called rootless cosmopolitanism and nationalism unfurled. It could not have passed over the Jewish Autonomous Region. Massive arrests of well-known cultural workers, academics, and Party and state workers were undertaken." The captions went on like that: "persecution began," "purges were conducted," "books were removed," "connections with foreign organizations were discontinued." The was the Stalin-as-a-force-of-nature narrative.

The utter denial of human agency is the ultimate insult to survivors, but ninety-year-old Bekerman, the last living voluntary settler in Birobidzhan, was the only one to articulate this. I picked him up from the synagogue on a Saturday morning. A synagogue had been established in Birobidzhan in 1929, a small wooden building constructed by some of the first settlers. Twenty years later, everyone who attended the Rosh Hashanah services was arrested; the rabbi was sentenced to death. Jews returned to the wooden building in the late 1950s, but with the end of Khrushchev's Thaw, gathering there became too risky again and services moved to private apartments. In the 1970s, when the air in the Soviet Union once more grew a bit lighter, services at the synagogue resumed.

But the last of the occasionally observant Jews were old, and by the mid-1980s a minyan—a quorum of ten Jewish adults—became impossible. The wooden building was repurposed. There was no synagogue in the Jewish Autonomous Region for the next twenty years—until American Jews had given enough money to erect two small stone buildings on Lenin Street, one for the synagogue and one for the Freud Jewish community center, both protected by a single metal fence.

The morning I met Bekerman at the synagogue, he had just attended services for Simchat Torah—the highest holiday of the year for Soviet Jews of my generation. On that day, hundreds of people would dance in the street in front of the central Moscow synagogue; we would shield our faces ineffectually from the secret police and Komsomol informers, out in force with their cameras, but still put our arms around one another and dance in circles to old Yiddish tunes, which we belted out ourselves. The Birobidzhan synagogue, however, is essentially an American import, with a young Lubavitcher rabbi who probably knows nothing of the peculiar traditions of secular Soviet Jews.

"He wanted us to cover our heads," Bekerman grumbled as we walked the fifteen yards to Freud. "What does he think? He thinks I believe in God?"

He waited for me to take the bait. I waited for him to continue. We studied each other. He was so tiny it was hard to believe that real old-man clothes could have been made for him. His eyes were largely obscured by cataracts, but he walked confidently enough, and I sensed that he could see me better than I might have thought. His lower lip was permanently rolled out, shiny and purplish. His hands were disproportionately large, with cracked, disintegrating yellowed nails, and once we were seated in the community center, he slid the fingers of his right hand along the edge of the table with a grating sound when he was nervous. He was a tiny shell of an old man, and this shell was filled with emotion, so strong and so raw I thought it might just be pure will to live.

"I go to synagogue," he explained to me, apparently angry at how little I seemed to understand, "because I like to read and I like to study. But

God? I cannot believe in God. Where was your God when the Jewish people were killed? When my parents and my five brothers and sisters were buried alive? You say he chose the Jewish people? He forsook the Jewish people!"

The difference between me and ninety-year-old Bekerman was that I had heard this before. He had not. He might have said it a few times, but the opportunities would have been few. There might be a synagogue and a community center in Birobidzhan, but there was still no place in the Jewish Autonomous Region to talk about the Jewish people and what had happened to them.

On one of my days in the city, I took a taxi across the Bira River, to the slums of Birobidzhan, where inebriated creatures of indeterminate age and gender wandered among the remaining wooden barracks. My destination was the film archive, where I would pick up a reconstituted copy of a 1937 propaganda film with Mikhoels's closest ally, the actor Benjamin Zuskin (executed in 1952), in the starring role. In the film, called *In Search of Happiness*, Zuskin portrays an American Jew who shuns the collective farm to look for gold—and comes to no good—while his wife leaves him for the collective farm and a Russian man. It is one of the most unappealing portrayals of anyone and anyplace that I have ever seen, and I cannot imagine whose idea of propaganda it could have reflected.

The director of the film archive, a sixtyish heavyset woman with dyed blond hair, had no desire to discuss the film. But she said she had things to tell me. Sitting behind her pressboard desk, she juggled several telephone headsets in her hands, shuffling papers at the same time, as though she had been looking for something important to show me. After a few minutes, she let her hands rest, looked at me, and said what she had to say in a very loud, very clear voice.

"Things are fine here," she declared sternly, though I had said nothing to suggest otherwise. "I like my city, I like my country, I like my family. In other countries, people like to talk about being Jewish. But here"—she looked straight at me, and her voice grew even louder—"we don't like to talk about it!"

As we talked, it emerged that this woman was not Jewish. Like many ethnic Russian Birobidzhan families, however, hers had mixed with the Jews. The woman's son was married to one of Iosif Bekerman's many granddaughters. All of Bekerman's three children were married to ethnic Russians, but his favorite granddaughter, Iosif had told me, smiling with his cataract-clouded eyes, strongly identified as Jewish. Yulia "even went to Jewish study classes," he related, in the big city of Khabarovsk, where she was studying to be a dentist. "Imagine that!" he said. "She told me she would always keep the name, she would always be a Bekerman." The month Yulia graduated from dental school, about six months before I visited Birobidzhan, she had also gotten married, to an ethnic Russian. As her wedding date neared, Iosif sensed doubts and finally decided to talk to his granddaughter. "I said to her, 'Take his name.' I said, 'You are going to have to live among people, you are going to have to work. You are not going to want to be a Bekerman.'" From what I could tell, Yulia had been relieved; she took her husband's Russian surname and was now living in Khabarovsk, working as a dentist, and saving for an apartment, and her grandfather was very proud of her.

The question everyone asked me before I went to Birobidzhan and after I returned was: Are there any Jews in the Jewish Autonomous Region? I posed it to Valery Gurevich, the deputy governor responsible for everything Jewish in the region, from the children's song-and-dance ensemble to the statues of imaginary shtetl figures all over the city—a series of illustrations to Sholem Aleichem stories cast in bronze. I felt ridiculous asking a Jew in Birobidzhan if there were Jews in Birobidzhan, but he was a master at answering this question. His answer was "Well . . ."

He tried to avoid giving me any figures at all—I had to fill them in later—but the gist of his story was this: Before the Soviet Union collapsed, the census placed the percentage of Jews in the Jewish Autonomous Region at a bit over four, which was about four times the percentage of Jews in the general population of the Soviet Union. In absolute figures, that was about nine thousand Jews. But these figures were based on answers people gave to the census taker, an official, in a country where if one had a choice (for example, if one of one's parents was not Jewish), one did not choose to call oneself Jewish. Just ten years before the last Soviet census, the percentage of Jews in the region's population had been three times higher—suggesting that it had been diluted by intermarriage but the number of people who had some Jewish roots was a lot higher than the official nine thousand.

So it should come as no surprise that the number of people who emigrated to Israel when this became possible, at the turn of the 1990s, far exceeded the official number of Jews in Birobidzhan. And there were still some Jews left—a couple thousand, give or take as many.

Of them, roughly five people—including Iosif Bekerman, Maria Rak, and Valery Gurevich—were engaged on an ongoing basis with Jewish culture. Of them, only one—Bekerman—spoke Yiddish. There were no Yiddish writers left in the Jewish Autonomous Region.

EPILOGUE

On February 18, 1981, my parents, my six-year-old brother, and I boarded a plane in Moscow. We had stayed up all night, in accordance with something that had become a tradition: departing émigrés held open houses all night before leaving. Dozens of people came to say good-bye, and I remember that my parents felt socially successful perhaps for the first and only time in their lives—throwing a going-away-forever party is as close as most of us can come to attending our own wakes. I also remember that some people did not come, evidently for fear of being associated with traitors to the Soviet motherland. Thirty-five years later, I recall their names but not the names of the people who were there.

By morning the festivities had grown bleary-eyed and the jokes tedious. There was one that I found increasingly unfunny, courtesy of a colleague and friend of my mother's, a man who would emigrate years later. "How do you know that the decadent West really exists?" he would ask. By "decadent West" he meant simply the West but as seen from the Soviet Union, where propaganda conventions dictated always adding that appellation. "Have you seen any material evidence of the decadent West's existence?" We had not, not really, aside from a few paperbacks, bubble gum, a couple of bottles of Pepsi, an impossibly perfect Bic pen owned by one of my classmates, and a set of bright plastic toothbrushes with absurdly large heads for improbably large white teeth, a gift from a visitor only my father had seen. This evidence was circumstantial at best, and inconclusive.

We were searched at the airport, under ruthless fluorescent lights. The customs officer decreed that my drawings had to stay in the country, along with my box of pencils and paper, but not an inlaid brooch from my great-grandmother, which I would soon lose myself. My little brother's yellow plastic gun was scrutinized. My relatives and a few of my parents' friends waved tirelessly from behind a steel barrier. A bus took us to a Vienna-bound plane.

The plane's destination was part of an elaborate charade. Our exit visas—small sheets of greenish-white paper, folded to make a book of three pages—were now our only identity documents, since we had been stripped of our Soviet citizenship as a condition of leaving. Fittingly, when we forfeited our Soviet passports, we lost the only identity documents that would list our *nationality* as Jewish—it was our citizenship that had been Soviet. Now we were "stateless" in the eyes of the world, though the visas said we were leaving the Soviet Union to go to Israel to take up permanent residence there.

The right to leave had been won, through hard work, by the joint efforts of Soviet Zionists and their supporters in the United States, but by the time it had been granted, in the early 1970s, the Soviet Union had long severed diplomatic ties with Israel. This meant, among other things, that a plane could not go directly from the Soviet Union to Israel, and neither could the Jews. Vienna, the nearest capitalist—Western—city to Moscow, became the way station. For the many beneficiaries of the right to leave who were not Zionists, this layover was a stroke of luck, a chance to break ranks and declare their intention to seek asylum in the United States—or Canada, or Australia, or, for the reckless and hopeless few, a Western European country that would never accept them. My parents were planning to take this option in Vienna, as were most of the people on our plane.

It was a plane full of people with one-way tickets and nothing to show for themselves but the greenish exit visas and one suitcase per person. The concentration of loss and hope made the air in the cabin feel thick. The plane sat on the runway for what seemed like hours. Would it ever take off? Did the West actually exist? I looked out the window, ready to watch the snowed-under landscape of my homeland recede in the gray morning light, but we sat and sat on the runway, and my supply of anticipatory nostalgia slowly evaporated.

A black Volga, an elegant Soviet rip-off of the classic Volvo, pulled up to the plane. Every refugee inside tensed, all of us gripping our exit visas. In terrified silence, we observed as two uniformed men exited the car, flanking a prison-pale man in black. By the time they had climbed the stairs into the cabin, someone's whispered "Mendelevich" had spread from head to tail. When they entered, I saw that the pale man was handcuffed to each of his uniformed companions. They released him, he sat down, they exited, and soon the plane took off.

All of us owed our right to leave the Soviet Union in large part to Yosef Mendelevich, the man who was now flying with us. In 1970, Mendelevich led a group of Jews in an effort to hijack a plane in order to fly to Sweden, where they planned to ask for help in getting to Israel. The group never got off the ground, or even on the plane—they were arrested near the airport hours before the planned hijacking. All of them were sentenced to long prison terms, and most were eventually released into foreign custody. Mendelevich had served nearly eleven years before he boarded our plane, which would take him to Vienna and from there to Israel. My parents' plan to tell the Israeli officials in Vienna that they did not want to make aliyah had just grown that much harder: they would have to do it in proximity to, and possibly in the presence of, a man who had risked all and sacrificed more than a decade of his life for their right to move to the Jewish homeland. (My parents still carried out their plan, in spite of considerable, and unsubtle, pressure from the Israelis in Vienna.)

Mendelevich was twenty-two years old when he attempted to hijack that plane. For several years before that, he had spent his Sundays in the Rumbula Forest outside Riga, as part of a small group of Jews cleaning up the place where tens of thousands of Jews had been executed—and on the way to which Dubnow had died. In 1964, the Jewish activists of Riga won the right to place a large stone on the site. It was the only monument to victims of the Holocaust erected in the Soviet Union, and the authorities had made their permission contingent on two requirements: the monument had to include Soviet state symbols, and it could not contain the word "Jewish." The large piece of black granite bore the words "To the victims of fascism" in Latvian, Russian, and Hebrew, and, on the other side, featured a hammer and sickle and the dates "1941–1944." It was consistent with the Soviet narrative, in which Hitler's victims had been the "anti-fascists."

Mendelevich and a small group of young Jews began not only to meet at Rumbula on Sundays but to form a group Jewish identity, for the first time since their parents' and grandparents' generations had been massacred in that forest. They also made contact with the few surviving representatives of those generations and learned about Zionism from them.[1] The plot to hijack an airplane took shape and, even in its failure, became one of the most important events of the new movement for Jewish emigration from the Soviet Union. That evening in February 1981, all of the passengers of our plane had dinner in a large hall at a refugee camp in Vienna. Mendelevich wore a wide-brimmed black hat, and his black clothes and his paleness now read as Orthodox rather than "prison."

The American Jews who had lobbied for Mendelevich to be released from prison, and for all of us to be released from the Soviet Union, expected every one of us to look like that—as if we had emerged from a turn-of-the-century family photograph, as if we had been perfectly preserved at Ellis Island for seventy-five years. Their Jewish identities began with those old photographs and vague stories of their forebears coming from someplace in what may or may not have been Russia.

To me, being Jewish was the shape of my nose, the color of my eyes and my hair, and the notation in my documents, all of which kept me from being like other people. For my parents, it was the source of their greatest fear—that their children would be kept from becoming who they could be and, more immediately and more to the point, that their children would get hurt. My parents knew precisely what they feared: both of them had been blindsided by college admissions committees that had rejected them for being Jewish. For both of them, Jewish was what they were and what they did not want to be.

When I was in my early teens, my mother's dinner-party conversation with a near stranger accidentally dispatched me to a clandestine festival of Jewish song held in a forest outside of Moscow. Attendees took a commuter train out to the designated station, then walked for a while, following discreet signs pinned to trees or drawn with a stick in the sandy ground, until the woods thickened and then opened into a clearing. There we laid down some logs to form an auditorium; we sat, and the space in front of us became the stage. Men and women, very young and just young, single, in couples, and in trios, usually with a guitar or two or three, took turns standing in front of the small crowd and singing. Their repertoire was limited: "Hava Nagila," "Tum Balalaika," "Shalom Aleichem"—in slightly varied arrangements and invariably passionate renderings. I had never heard any of these songs before, yet I felt that I had grown up listening to them. For the first time in my life, I felt that I belonged to a community of people.

When we arrived in the United States, the Jewish community in Boston assigned us to a well-meaning suburban family to help us in the acculturation process. Our relationship with them played out in accordance with a scenario followed by tens of thousands of pairings of Jewish families around the United States in the 1970s and 1980s. They were nice. They wanted to celebrate Shabbat with us and help us find our way to a synagogue. They wanted to facilitate my belated bat mitzvah and my brother's bar mitzvah, this one in a timely manner, God willing. All my parents wanted was the option, finally, of not being Jewish. I wanted something marginally more complicated: unlimited access to Yiddish musical schlock.

Decades later, I read Mendelevich's interviews about groping in the dark for any information about being Jewish, collecting scraps of holiday traditions and music. His path had begun in the Rumbula Forest.[2] Later still, I read Simon Dubnow, who was shot in his old age for being too slow to walk to the Rumbula Forest. Dubnow finally released me from thinking that our community-assigned mentors had been more Jewish than I was.

And what of the place where Dubnow's autonomist vision should have been realized? It was the least Jewish of all. In the Sholem Aleichem Library, in Birobidzhan, in the tiny room that houses what the library describes as the "national collection," I found a single book published in Yiddish, in the 1990s. Printed on the cheap paper that carried so many important words in that decade, it is a poetry collection, a bilingual Russian-Yiddish edition. Good poetry is always a surprise, and a couple of the poems struck me and stayed with me. I tracked down the author.

I would have wanted to pass the baton to my sons,
a symbol of our shared grief and our shared pain.
Not a symbol of victories
nor a candy or a wrapper
but a symbol of pain, a symbol of war
in which I did not die.
I was an unforgivably bad soldier in this war,
and I deserve no medals. I don't even deserve sympathy.
I have betrayed my era
because I lived, like a mouse, in the cellar of silence.
Never mind the era: I
betrayed my own father,
My father, who never returned from the other world war.
I've betrayed everyone who did not come home in the 1930s,
everyone who turned to dust, to grass, to trees.
I would have liked to pass the baton to my sons,
but I have nothing to pass on,
save for the grief, the pain, and the happiness I lack,
and the belief that I can still find it.

"It's about growing up Soviet," Leonid Shkolnik, the poet, told me when we met. "Nothing else, just Soviet. We knew nothing else." Shkolnik's father died while a soldier in the Soviet army at the very end of the Second World War; Leonid himself, conceived during his father's New Year's furlough, was born after the war. When he was a small child, his mother moved their family of two to Birobidzhan, where she had a sister—the Shkolniks' only surviving relative. Shkolnik's mother worked as an accountant. He went to School Number Two, where most of the students were ethnic Jews and no one ever talked about it. The first time he recalled anyone asking him if he was Jewish was when he was ten or eleven and two Israelis stopped him in the street. That would have been the 1956 visit by the Avidars, the Israeli ambassador and his wife. They gave the boy some Israeli stamps; like many Soviet schoolchildren, he collected these tokens of other countries' existence.

He told me that it was perhaps this encounter that prompted him, a few years later, to ask his mother to teach him Yiddish; he had heard her speaking the half-forbidden language to her sister. He became the youngest Yiddish speaker in Birobidzhan. And since he also wrote poetry, he fell in with the crowd of Yiddish-language poets—the ones who had been jailed when he was a toddler. They now groomed Shkolnik to become the editor of *Birobidzhaner shtern*.

He thought of himself as a freethinker; indeed, he was so independent of authority that he sometimes published truncated versions of Politburo members' speeches—the censorship bureau did not have anyone who spoke Yiddish, so no one could check his copy. Otherwise, editing the newspaper was an adventureless enterprise, and it hardly occurred to Shkolnik to question whether this should be so. "I was a Soviet person," he told me. "The whole country condemned Zionist aggression—and we condemned it, too. The paper absolutely had to do it; this was a nonnegotiable part of my job. And the thing is, this was not a trade-off for me—it's not like I consciously promoted a position I did not support in order to work for the paper; I actually believed it."

One time—it must have been in the mid-1980s—Shkolnik saw an old Birobidzhan character, an aging man who went hatless year-round, reading the most recent issues of *Birobidzhaner shtern* on an outdoor billboard. (All Soviet papers were regularly posted on such billboards.) Shkolnik approached him, fishing for a compliment. "This is all crap, the stuff you write," the man snapped. "You are marching to the orders of TASS [the

Telegraph Agency of the Soviet Union]; all the papers print the same thing." Then he told Shkolnik that he had served time in the camps, and that was when he had stopped wearing a hat. "Because that's how the guards tortured us, in minus-sixty weather, making us work hatless in lumber production. When we relieved ourselves, our urine froze. So the weather in Birobidzhan is nothing for me." The man had spent years trying to get permission to emigrate, and he died in Birobidzhan.

By the late 1980s, Shkolnik was one of the best-known people in Birobidzhan. When the Soviet Union held its first quasi-free election, he ran for parliament on a platform of securing greater autonomy for Birobidzhan and restoring Yiddish-language book publishing. He was elected in 1989 and became, for the Soviet TV-watching public, the face of Birobidzhan.

In 1990, Shkolnik traveled to Israel with a small Soviet parliamentary delegation; diplomatic relations between the two countries had not been restored yet. "I was shocked," he told me. "I loved everything, including the fact that the signs are in Hebrew and there are orange trees growing along the sides of the road, and when I returned to Birobidzhan, I wrote about this. The chief architect of the city immediately wrote a letter saying I was lying and that in fact there was barbed wire along the roads here."

Shkolnik became obsessed, and he finally used a contact in the Israeli intelligence services to have himself smuggled to Israel. A couple of months later, as the Soviet Union wound down and collapsed, emigration became a simple matter of buying a ticket. Thus the last of the Yiddish-language poets of Birobidzhan, the last of the many men who had promised to make it a Yiddish-reading autonomy, also became the last Russian Jew to have expended extraordinary effort in order to emigrate to Israel.

ACKNOWLEDGMENTS

For a little book, this one took a long time and a lot of human effort. I am indebted to Jonathan Rosen, then of Nextbook, who assigned this book back in ancient times. At Knopf, editor Dan Frank rescued the book, an earlier version of which was languishing. My agent, Elyse Cheney, prodded me to listen to Dan, which was one of the best things I've done: his guidance and his patience made it finally turn into a book. I am grateful to everyone who has talked with me about Jewish diaspora identity, emigration, and nationalisms—especially to Svetlana Boym, whose voice I miss every day. And as always, nothing I do is possible without Darya Oreshkina, who also, as is her way, created the maps and infographics for this book.

NOTES

Chapter 1

1. Zvi Gitelman, *A Century of Ambivalence: The Jews of Russia and the Soviet Union, 1881 to the Present* (Bloomington: Indiana University Press, 2001), 1–10.
2. Joseph Sherman, "David Bergelson (1884–1952): A Biography," in *David Bergelson: From Modernism to Socialist Realism*, edited by Joseph Sherman and Gennady Estraikh (London: Legenda, 2007), 7.
3. Sherman, 7.
4. Sherman, 8–10.
5. There are many ways to transcribe these writers' names, and they themselves changed transcriptions as they moved from language to language. I have opted for the transcriptions used by YIVO.

Chapter 2

1. Simon Dubnow, "The Doctrine of Jewish Nationalism," in Simon Dubnow, *Nationalism and History: Essays on Old and New Judaism*, ed. Koppel S. Pinson (Philadelphia: Jewish Publication Society of America, 1958).
2. Dubnow, 77.
3. Dubnow, 97.
4. Simon Dubnow, "Autonomism, the Basis of the National Program," in Dubnow, *Nationalism and History*, 131–142.
5. Simon Dubnow, "Reality and Fantasy in Zionism," in Dubnow, *Nationalism and History*, 155–166.
6. Theodor Herzl, *The Jewish State* (CreateSpace Independent Publishing Platform, 2011), 2.
7. Sofia Dubnova-Erlich, *Zhizn i tvorchestvo S. M. Dubnova* (publication information unknown; obtained online), 118.
8. Simon Dubnow, "A Historic Moment (The Question of Emigration)," in Simon Dubnow, *Nationalism and History*, 192–99.
9. Dubnova-Erlich, 211.

10. Dubnova-Erlich. 234.
11. Timothy Snyder, *Black Earth: The Holocaust as History and Warning* (New York: Tim Duggan Books, 2015), 61.
12. Dubnova-Erlich. 238.
13. Dubnova-Erlich, 256–57.
14. Dubnova-Erlich, 258.
15. Dubnova-Erlich, 266.
16. Dubnova-Erlich, 267.
17. Dubnova-Erlich, 271.
18. Simon Dubnow, "The Emancipation Movement and the Emigration Movement," in Dubnow, *Nationalism and History*, 233–52.

Chapter 3

1. Joshua Rubenstein and Vladimir P. Naumov, *Stalin's Secret Pogrom: The Postwar Inquisition of the Jewish Anti-Fascist Committee*, abridged edition (New Haven: Yale University Press, 2005), 127.
2. Lev Bergelson, "Memories of My Father: The Early Years (1918–1934)," in *David Bergelson*, ed. Joseph Sherman and Gennady Estraikh (London: Legenda, 2007), 79.
3. Zvi Gitelman, *A Century of Ambivalence: The Jews of Russia and the Soviet Union, 1881 to the Present* (Bloomington: Indiana University Press, 2001), 65–70.
4. Lev Bergelson, 79.
5. "The Founding Tasks of the Kultur-Lige," in Simon Rabinovitch, ed., *Jews and Diaspora Nationalism: Writings on Jewish Peoplehood in Europe and the United States* (Waltham, MA: Brandeis, 2012), 143.
6. David E. Fishman, *The Rise of Modern Yiddish Culture* (Pittsburgh: University of Pittsburgh Press, 2005), 83.
7. Sherman, 24.
8. Lev Bergelson, 80.
9. Gitelman, 76–77.
10. Lev Bergelson, 80.
11. Sherman, 25.
12. Sherman, 25.
13. Lev Bergelson, 81.
14. Simon Dubnow, *Kniga zhizni. Materialy dlya istorii moyego vremeni* (Jerusalem, Moscow: Hesharim/Mosty Kultury; 2004), 526.
15. Sherman, 26.
16. Sherman, 25.
17. Dubnow, *Kniga zhizni*, 526–33.
18. Gennadi Estraikh, *In Harness: Yiddish Writers' Romance with Communism* (Syracuse, NY: Syracuse University Press, 2005), 68.

19. Sherman, 26.
20. Lev Bergelson, 85.
21. Ellen Kellman, "Bergelson at Forverts," in *David Bergelson: From Modernism to Socialist Realism*, ed. Joseph Sherman and Gennady Estraikh (London: Legenda, 2007), 198.
22. Sherman, 35.
23. Dubnow, *Kniga zhizni*, 532.
24. Dubnow, *Kniga zhizni*, 539.
25. Gennady Estraikh, "David Bergelson in and on America (1929–1949)," in Sherman and Estraikh, eds., *David Bergelson*, 205.
26. Dubnow, *Kniga zhizni*, 533.
27. Kellman, 190.
28. Kellman, 191.
29. Quoted in Sherman, 36.

Chapter 4

1. Sherman, 38.
2. Kellman, 192.
3. Kellman, 194.
4. Kellman, 192.
5. Estraikh, 78–79.
6. Kellman, 192.
7. Kellman, 200.

Chapter 5

1. Sherman, 41.
2. Sherman, 42.
3. Gennady Estraikh in Sherman and Estraikh, eds., *David Bergelson*, 210–11.
4. Estraikh, in *David Bergelson*, 212.
5. Estraikh, in *David Bergelson*, 214.
6. Anita Shapira, *Land and Power: The Zionist Resort to Force, 1881–1948* (Stanford: Stanford University Press, 1999), 173–74.
7. Tareq Y. Ismael, *The Communist Movement in the Arab World* (New York: RoutledgeCurzon, 2005), 61.
8. Estraikh, in *David Bergelson*, 212–13.
9. Lev Bergelson, 88.
10. Estraikh, in *David Bergelson*, 206.
11. Sherman, 50.

Chapter 6

1. Quoted in Terry Martin, *The Affirmative Action Empire: Nations and Nationalism in the Soviet Union, 1923–1939* (Ithaca: Cornell University Press, 2001), 44.
2. Quoted in O. P. Zhuravleva, *Istoriya knizhnogo dela v yevreskoy aftonomnoy oblasti (konets 1920-kh—nachalo 1960-kh godov)* (Khabarovsk: Dalnevostochnaya Gosudarstvennaya Biblioteka, 2008), 37.
3. Quoted in Zhuravleva, 38.
4. B. L. Bruk, *Predvaritelniy svodniy otchet expeditsii KOMZETa v 1927 godu*, ed. V. R. Viliams (Moscow: n.p., 1928).
5. Documents from the permanent exhibit of the Birobidzhan Regional Museum, viewed October 4–8, 2009.
6. "Birobidzhan glazami amerikanskogo zhurnalista Davida Brauna," documents from the State Archives of Birobidzhan reproduced by Freud, the Birobidzhan Jewish community center, 10.
7. Boris Kotlerman, "The Construction of the Jewish Space: Immigrant Settlements in Birobidzhan," in Ber Boris Kotlerman and Shmuel Yavin, *Bauhaus in Birobidzhan: 80 Years of Jewish Settlement in the Far East of the USSR* (Tel Aviv: Bauhaus Center, 2008), 128.
8. Iosif Brener, *Lehaim, Birobidzhan!* (Krasnoyarsk: Krasnoyarsky Pisatel, 2007), 25–28.
9. "Vospominaniya pervyh pereselentsev," documents from the State Archives of Birobidzhan reproduced by Freud, the Birobidzhan Jewish community center, recollections of Leyba Refoels Shkolnik, 11–12.
10. "Vospominaniya," 13.

Chapter 7

1. Boris Kotlerman, "'Why I Am in Favour of Birobidzhan': Bergelson's Fateful Decision (1932)," in Sherman and Estraikh, eds., *David Bergelson*, 223–24.
2. Sherman, 51.
3. Estraikh in Sherman and Estraikh, eds., *David Bergelson*, 215.
4. Rubenstein and Naumov, 131.
5. Sherman, 51.

Chapter 8

1. Rubenstein and Naumov, 131–32.
2. Kotlerman and Yavin, 140–42.
3. Brown's dispatch, published January 6, 1933, reverse-translated from Russian according to "Birobidzhan glazami," 14.
4. "Birobidzhan glazami," 10.

5. David A. Brown, "Final Conclusions on the Matter of the Soviet Dream of the Construction of Birobidzhan," *American Hebrew and Jewish Tribune*, January 20, 1933, reverse translation according to "Birobidzhan glazami," 23–24.

6. David Bergelson, "Birobidzhanskiye motivy," in David Bergelson, *Izbranniye proizvedeniya* (Moscow: OGIZ, Der Emes, 1947), 329–30. The story was originally written in Yiddish and later translated into Russian by Bergelson. I translated this excerpt from the Russian version.

7. Zhuravleva, 47.

8. Zhuravleva, 111.

9. B. Miller, "Nachalo," in *Vospominaniya o Em. Kazakeviche*, ed. G. O. Kazakevich and B. S. Ruben (Moscow: Sovetsky Pisatel, 1984), 54.

10. G. G. Kazakevich, "Nemnogo o nashey semye," in Kazakevich and Ruben, eds., *Vospominaniya*, 21.

11. Yakov Chernis, "V tayezhnom krayu," in Kazakevich and Ruben, eds., *Vospominaniya*, 59–60.

12. Lyubov Vasserman, "Dve vstrechi," in Kazakevich and Ruben, eds., *Vospominaniya*, 56–57.

13. The incident is described by Vasserman in Kazakevich and Ruben, eds., *Vospominaniya*, 57–58.

14. Quoted in Kotlerman in Sherman and Estraikh, eds., *David Bergelson*, 225.

15. Rubenstein and Naumov, 131.

16. Podstrochnik, *Zhizn' Lilianny Lunginoy, rasskazannaya yeyu v fil'me Olega Dormana* (Moscow: Corpus, 2009), 65–66.

Chapter 9

1. Sherman in Sherman and Estraikh, eds., *David Bergelson*, 52.

2. Kotlerman in Sherman and Estraikh, eds., *David Bergelson*, 229–30.

3. Kotlerman in Sherman and Estraikh, eds., *David Bergelson*, 230.

4. Zhuravleva, 75.

5. Nora Levin, *Paradox of Survival: The Jews in the Soviet Union Since 1917*, vol. 1 (New York: New York University Press, 1990), 302.

6. Kotlerman and Yavin, 124.

7. Kotlerman and Yavin, 141.

8. "1936 Constitution of the Union of Soviet Socialist Republics," http://www .hrono.ru/dokum/193_dok/cnst1936.html#7; accessed November 14, 2009.

9. Kotlerman and Yavin, 141.

10. Quoted in Levin, 303.

11. Birobidzhan Regional Museum, permanent exhibition.

12. T. Gen, "Yego lubili," in Kazakevich and Ruben, eds., *Vospominaniya*, 43.

13. Quoted in Levin, 307.

14. Birobidzhan Regional Museum.

15. Levin, 307.

16. Levin, 307.
17. Zhuravleva, 80.
18. Levin, 308.
19. Zhuravleva, 80.
20. Zhuravleva, 345.
21. Quoted in Levin, 308.
22. Sherman, 56.
23. Levin, 327.
24. Kotlerman in Sherman and Estraikh, eds., *David Bergelson*, 228–30.
25. Interview with Leonid Shkolnik, Jerusalem, November 2009.
26. Birobidzhan Regional Museum.
27. A telegram confirming the arrest and the placement of children in state custody is on display as part of the permanent exhibit at the Birobidzhan Regional Museum.
28. Robert Weinberg, *Stalin's Forgotten Zion: Birobidzhan and the Making of a Soviet Jewish Homeland; An Illustrated History, 1928–1996* (Berkeley: University of California Press, 1998), 67.
29. Yuri Slezkine, *The Jewish Century* (Princeton: Princeton University Press), 274–97.
30. Stepan Laletin, Birobidzhan Museum exhibit.
31. Yuri Kosvintsev, Birobidzhan Museum exhibit.
32. Fedor Vayser, Birobidzhan Museum.
33. Lazar Bimets, Birobidzhan Museum.
34. Nikolay Blagoy, Birobidzhan Museum.
35. Valdheym Museum, permanent exhibit.
36. Weinberg, 67.
37. Birobidzhan Regional Museum.
38. Kotlerman in Sherman and Estraikh, eds., *David Bergelson*, 230.
39. Kotlerman and Yavin, 143.
40. Zhuravleva, 56–67.
41. Birobidzhan Regional Museum.
42. Zhuravleva, 106–08.
43. Kotlerman in Sherman and Estraikh, eds., *David Bergelson*, 231

Chapter 10

1. Text of the Molotov-Ribbentrop Pact, http://legacy.fordham.edu/halsall/mod/1939pact.html; accessed August 24, 2015.
2. Kotlerman and Yavin, 140.
3. Memoir by actor David Lederman quoted in Rubenstein and Naumov, 6–7.
4. Interview with David Markish, son of Perets Markish, at http://www.languages-study.com/yiddish/markishsons.html; accessed December 2, 2009.
5. Dubnova-Erlich, 277.

6. The Riga Ghetto and Latvian Holocaust Museum, permanent exhibition.
7. Koppel S. Pinson, introduction to Dubnow, *Nationalism and History.*
8. Museum of the Occupation of Latvia, permanent exhibit.
9. Dubnova-Erlich, 278.

Chapter 11

1. Rubenstein and Naumov, 7–8.
2. Shimon Redlich, K. M. Anderson, and I. Al'tman, *War, Holocaust, and Stalinism: A Documented History of the Jewish Anti-Fascist Committee in the USSR* (Luxembourg: Harwood Academic), 174.
3. Rubenstein and Naumov, 8–9.
4. "Rech I.V. Stalina po radio 3 iyula 1941 goda," https://www.youtube.com/watch?v=duAdhke98xU; accessed February 1, 2016.
5. David Shneer, "From Mourning to Vengeance: Bergelson's Holocaust Journalism (1941–1945)," in Sherman and Estraikh, eds., *David Bergelson,* 252.
6. Quoted in Sherman, in Sherman and Estraikh, eds., *David Bergelson,* 57.
7. Reproduced in Redlich, 175.
8. Hannah Arendt, *Eichmann in Jerusalem: A Report on the Banality of Evil,* revised and enlarged edition (New York: Penguin, 1994), 78–90.
9. Arendt, 78.
10. David S. Wyman, *The Abandonment of the Jews: America and the Holocaust, 1941–1945* (New York: Pantheon, 1985), 20.
11. Anatoly Kuznetsov, *Baby Yar* (Moscow: Astrel, 2010).
12. Shneer, 253.
13. Reproduced in Redlich, 186.
14. Kuznetsov, 116–119, 127.
15. Quoted in Shneer, 251.

Chapter 12

1. Quoted in Shneer, 253.
2. Quoted in Shneer, 259.
3. Quoted in Shneer, 260.
4. Quoted in Sherman, in Sherman and Estraikh, eds., *David Bergelson,* 65.
5. Quoted in Sherman, in Sherman and Estraikh, eds., *David Bergelson,* 64.
6. Quoted in Shneer, 262–64.
7. Ilya Altman, "Beliye pyatna 'Chernoy knigi,'" at http://www.lechaim.ru/ARHIV/124/poznansk.htm; accessed December 15, 2009.
8. Ilya Ehrenburg, *Lyudi, gody, zhizn,* vol. 2 (Moscow: Sovetsky Pisatel, 1990), 358.
9. Altman.
10. Ehrenburg, 358.

Chapter 13

1. Rubenstein and Naumov, 18.
2. Rubenstein and Naumov, 18–19.
3. Israel Emiot, *The Birobidzhan Affair: A Yiddish Writer in Siberia* (Philadelphia: The Jewish Publication Society of America, 1981), 4.
4. Moyshe Tsekhtik, "V yevreyskom detskom dome," http://shkolnik08.livejournal .com/20576.html; accessed October 7, 2009.
5. Sergo Bengelsdorf, "Birobidzhan kakim ya yego pomnyu," http://shkolnik08 .livejournal.com/18476.html; accessed October 7, 2009.
6. Leonid Shkolnik, "Lyuba Vasserman: Arest i posle nego," unpublished manuscript.
7. "Otchet o priyeme, razmeshenii i hozyaystvennogo [*sic*] ustroystva [*sic*] pereselentsev za 1949 god," signed by S. Livshits and dated January 31, 1950.

Chapter 14

1. V. P. Naumov, ed., *Nepravedny sud: Posledniy Stalinskiy rasstrel* (Moscow: Nauka, 1994), 5.
2. Rubenstein and Naumov, 1.
3. Naumov, 6–7.
4. Vayserman, *Birobidzhan: Mechty I tragediya* (Khabarovsk: RIOTIP, 1999), 372.
5. Naumov, 82.
6. Rubenstein and Naumov, XII–XIII (with a single correction of the translation: Rubenstein translates *besposhaden* as "pitiless," while I believe "merciless" is more accurate).
7. Indictment filed in the JAC case retrieved on December 21, 2009: http://www .hrono.ru/dokum/195_dok/19520403_eak.html.
8. Penal code of the RSFSR retrieved on December 21, 2009: http://stalinism.ru /Dokumentyi/Statya-58-UK-RSFSR.html.
9. Naumov, 11.
10. Naumov, 11.

Chapter 15

1. Vayserman, 372, 377.
2. Vayserman, 374.
3. Vayserman, 278–82.
4. Vayserman, 302.
5. Vayserman, 315.
6. Vayserman, 317.

7. Vayserman, 294.
8. Vayserman, 324–25.

Chapter 16

1. Vayserman, 357.
2. Vayserman, 359.
3. Tsekhtik.
4. Vayserman, 354.
5. Bekerman interview, Birobidzhan, October 2009.
6. Vayserman, 378.
7. Vayserman, 382.
8. Vayserman, 379.

Chapter 17

1. Naumov, 18.
2. Naumov, 21.
3. Naumov, 23–29.
4. A letter by Mikhoels and Fefer to the Central Committee, retrieved on December 22, 2009: http://www.loc.gov/exhibits/archives/m2antfac.html.
5. Naumov, 64–65.
6. Naumov, 71.

Chapter 18

1. Naumov, 75–89.
2. Naumov, 381–84.
3. Naumov, 388–93.

Chapter 19

1. Cited in Weinberg, 85.
2. Interview with Leonid Shkolnik, Jerusalem, November 2009.

Chapter 20

1. Bumagin Iosif Romanovich, biography retrieved on January 5, 2010: http://www.warheroes.ru/hero/hero.asp?Hero_id=4758.

Epilogue

1. Gal Beckerman, *When They Come for Us, We'll Be Gone: The Epic Struggle to Save Soviet Jewry* (New York: Houghton Mifflin Harcourt, 2010), 13–38.
2. Judy Lash Balint, *Jerusalem Diaries II: What's Really Happening in Israel* (Longwood, FL: Xulon, 2007), 35.

Endpapers

Climate: Roshydromet, Israel Meteorological Service.

Type of Lands: Report of Giprvod expedition, 1931 (State Archive of Jewish Autonomous Region); Abram Merezhin, *O zaselenii Biro-Bidzhanskogo raiona trudiashchimisia evreiami*, 1928; E. Mills, *Census of Palestine 1931*, vol. 1, p. 23 (Alexandria, 1933); A. Kantorovich, *Perspectivy Birobidzhana* (Moscow: Emes, 1932).

Change of Population: Census of Russia, 2010; Shlomo Groman, *Skol'ko evreev ostalos v Birobidzhane* (Novosti nedeli, February–March, 2005), www.languages-study.com/demography/birobijan.html; *Administrativno-territorial'noe ustroystvo Evreyskoy Avtonomnoy Oblasti, 1858–2003 gg* (Khabarovsk, 2004); *Razvitie Evreyskoy Avtonomnoy Oblasti*, www.eao.ru/?p=1462.

PUBLISHED SOURCES

Altman, Ilya. "Beliye pyatna 'Chernoy knigi.'" December 15, 2009. http://www
.lechaim.ru/ARHIV/124/poznansk.htm.
Arendt, Hannah. *Eichmann in Jerusalem: A Report on the Banality of Evil.* Revised and
enlarged edition. New York: Penguin, 1994.
Balint, Judy Lash. *Jerusalem Diaries II: What's Really Happening in Israel.* Longwood,
FL: Xulon, 2007.
Beckerman, Gal. *When They Come for Us, We'll Be Gone: The Epic Struggle to Save Soviet
Jewry.* Boston: Houghton Mifflin Harcourt, 2010.
Bengelsdorf, Sergo. "Birobidzhan kakim ya yego pomnyu." October 7, 2009. http://
shkolnik08.livejournal.com/18476.html.
Bergelson, David. *Izbranniye proizvedeniya.* Moscow: OGIZ, Der Emes, 1947.
———. *Mirele.* Moscow: OGIZ, Gosudarstvennoye izdatel'stvo khudozhestvennoy
literarury, 1941.
———. *Na Dnepre.* Moscow: Sovetsky pisatel, 1983.
Brener, Iosif. *Lehaim, Birobidzhan!* Krasnoyarsk: Krasnoyarsky Pisatel, 2007.
Bruk, B. L. *Predvaritelniy svodniy otchet expeditsii KOMZETa v 1927 godu.* Ed. V. R. Vil-
iams. Moscow: n.p., 1928.
Dubnova-Erlich, Sofia. *Zhizn' i tvorchestvo S. M. Dubnova* (publication information
unknown; obtained online).
Dubnow, Simon. *Kniga zhizni: Materialy dlia istorii moego vremeni. Vospominaniia I
razmyshleniia.* Jerusalem, Moscow: Hesharim/Mosty Kul'tury, 2004.
———. *Nationalism and History: Essays on Old and New Judaism.* Edited by Koppel S.
Pinson. Philadelphia: Jewish Publication Society of America, 1958.
Ehrenburg, Ilya. *Lyudi, gody, zhizn.* Vol. 2. Moscow: Sovetsky Pisatel, 1990.
Emiot, Israel. *The Birobidzhan Affair: A Yiddish Writer in Siberia.* Philadelphia: Jewish
Publication Society of America, 1981.
Estraikh, Gennady. *In Harness: Yiddish Writers' Romance with Communism.* Syracuse,
NY: Syracuse University Press, 2005.
Fishman, David E. *The Rise of Modern Yiddish Culture.* Pittsburgh: University of Pitts-
burgh, 2005.
Gitelman, Zvi. *A Century of Ambivalence: The Jews of Russia and the Soviet Union, 1881 to
the Present.* Bloomington: Indiana University Press, 2001.

Published Sources

Grossman, Vasily, and Ilya Ehrenburg, eds., *Chornaya kniga. O zlodeyskom povsemestnom ubiystve yevreyev nemetsko-fashistskimi zakhvatchikami vo vremenno okkupirovannykh rayonakh Sovetskogo Soyuza i v lageryakh Pol'shi vo vremya voyny 1941–1945 gg.* Vilnius: Yad, 1993.

Gurevich, V., Tsap, V. *O Yevreyskoy avtonomnoy oblasti—vseryoz i s ulybkoy.* Birobidzhan: Freud, 2009.

Herzl, Theodor. *The Jewish State.* N.p.: CreateSpace Independent Platform, 2011.

Kazakevich, G. O., and B. S. Ruben. *Vospominaniya o Em. Kazakeviche.* Ed. Moscow: Sovetsky Pisatel, 1984.

Kotlerman, Ber Boris, Shmuel Yavin, *Bauhaus in Birobidzhan: 80 Years of Jewish Settlement in the Far East of the USSR.* Tel Aviv: Merkaz Ba'uha'us, 2008.

Krishtofovich, A. N. and Z. A. Abdullayeva, eds., *Trudy Birobidzhanskoy geologicheskoy ekspeditsyi LenOZETa, 1933–1934 gg.* Leningrad and Moscow: Glavnaya redaktsiya gorno-toplivnoy literatury, 1937.

Kuznetsov, Anatoly. *Baby Yar.* Moscow: Astrel, 2010.

Levin, Nora. *Paradox of Survival: The Jews in the Soviet Union Since 1917.* Vol. 1. New York: New York University Press, 1990.

Martin, Terry. *The Affirmative Action Empire: Nations and Nationalism in the Soviet Union, 1923–1939.* Ithaca: Cornell University Press, 2001.

Melikhov, Alexander. *Birobidzhan—Zemlya obitovannaya.* Moscow: Tekst, 2009.

Miller, Boris. *Yasnost'.* Moscow: Sovetsky Pisatel, 1974.

"The Molotov-Ribbentrop Pact, 1939." *Modern History Sourcebook.* http://legacy.fordham.edu/halsall/mod/1939pact.html; accessed August 24, 2015.

Naumov, V. P., ed., *Nepravedny sud. Posledniy Stalinskiy rasstrel.* Moscow: Nauka, 1994.

Rabinovitch, Simon, ed., *Jews and Diaspora Nationalism: Writings on Jewish Peoplehood in Europe and the United States.* Waltham, MA: Brandeis University Press, 2012.

Rapoport, Louis. *Stalin's War Against the Jews: The Doctors' Plot and the Soviet Solution.* New York and Toronto: The Free Press, 1990.

Redlich, Shimon, K. M. Anderson, and I. Al'tman. *War, Holocaust, and Stalinism: A Documented Study of the Jewish Anti-Fascist Committee in the USSR.* Luxembourg: Harwood Academic, 1995.

Rubenstein, Joshua, and V. P. Naumov. *Stalin's Secret Pogrom: The Postwar Inquisition of the Jewish Anti-Fascist Committee.* Abridged edition. New Haven: Yale University Press, 2005.

Shapira, Anita. *Land and Power: The Zionist Resort to Force, 1881–1948.* Stanford: Stanford University Press, 1999.

Sherman, Joseph, and Gennady Estraikh. *David Bergelson: From Modernism to Socialist Realism.* London: Legenda, 2007.

Slezkine, Yuri. *The Jewish Century.* Princeton: Princeton University Press, 2006.

Snyder, Timothy. *Black Earth: The Holocaust as History and Warning.* New York: Tim Duggan Books, 2015.

Vayserman, David. *Birobidzhan. Mechty i tragediya.* Khabarovsk: RIOTIP, 1999.

Weinberg, Robert. *Stalin's Forgotten Zion: Birobidzhan and the Making of a Soviet Jew-*

ish Homeland; An Illustrated History, 1928–1996. Berkeley: University of California Press, 1998.

Wyman, David S. *The Abandonment of the Jews: America and the Holocaust, 1941–1945.* New York: Pantheon, 1985.

Zhuravleva, O. P. *Istoriya knizhnogo dela v Yevreskoy Avtonomnoy Oblasti (konets 1920-kh—nachalo 1960-kh godov).* Khabarovsk: Dalnevostochnaya Gosudarstvennaya Biblioteka, 2008.

INDEX

Aleichem, Sholem, 6, 8, 67, 126, 129, 138
Alexander II, Czar of Russia, 12
Alter, Wiktor, 26, 77–78, 85
American Hebrew and Jewish Tribune, 57
American Jewish Joint Distribution
　　Committee, 33–34
Amurzet farm, 51
anti-gay campaign, 11, 131
anti-Semitism
　　assassination of Alexander II and, 12
　　under Nazism, 26–27, 54–55
　　in Poland, 25–26
　　in post-Soviet Moscow, 10
　　in pre-revolutionary Russia, 22–23, 27,
　　　　29–31, 50
　　during the Russian Revolution,
　　　　29–31
　　in Russified Birobidzhan, 112–15
　　in the Soviet Union, 4–6, 63, 80, 95,
　　　　97–100, 125, 136, 144
　　Zionist response to, 21
"An Appeal to World Jewry," 81–82
Asch, Sholem, 89
autonomism, 6, 8
　　Dubnow's concept of, 18–29, 39–41,
　　　　145
　　early Soviet policies of, 37, 39–42,
　　　　47–52, 66
　　Great Terror purges and, 9, 68–71, 94,
　　　　100–125, 133–35
　　Ukraine's policies on, 30–31
Avidar, Yosef, 127–28, 146

Bakhmutsky, Alexander, 108–10
Bauhaus architecture, 66–67, 94
Bekerman, Iosif, 96–97, 99, 113–14, 130,
　　135–39
Bekerman, Yulia, 138
Bengelsdorf, Moshe, 95
Bergelson, David, 12–15, 133
　　advocacy for Yiddish literary culture
　　　　by, 31–36, 41–42, 65–71, 84
　　arrest and trial of, 101–6, 116–24
　　Communist Party jobs of, 32–33, 64
　　execution of, 124–25
　　flight from Birobidzhan of, 69–70
　　Great Terror denunciations by,
　　　　68–69, 119
　　Great Terror purges of writings of,
　　　　111, 116–21
　　honors and celebrations of, 71, 88
　　migrations of, 14–15, 29–38, 54–55,
　　　　120–21
　　pro-Soviet writing of, 40–46, 73, 88
　　returns to Soviet Union of, 39, 42–46,
　　　　53–55, 63–64
　　support of the Soviet war effort by,
　　　　79–91
　　visits to and promotion of
　　　　Birobidzhan by, 53–71, 93, 95
　　visit to New York by, 44–45
　　writing for New York's Yiddish
　　　　dailies by, 35–37, 40–42, 45
　　writing on the Holocaust by, 73–74,
　　　　85–90

Bergelson, David (*continued*)
  Yiddish fiction and plays of, 13–15, 37,
    44, 59–60, 83, 91
Bergelson, Lev, 30–31, 33, 46, 54
Bergelson, Tsipe Kutsenogaya, 29–30,
    32, 46, 63
Berlin
  interwar refugee population of, 34–35
  Jewish cultural life in, 24, 33–37, 121
  Jewish exodus from, 24–25
  rise of Nazism in, 26–27, 54–55
Bialik, Hayim Nahman, 19, 29, 32–33,
    36, 128
Bird's Milk group, 60
Birobidzhan, 5–11, 40, 129–39
  American sponsors of, 51, 57–59, 95, 136
  arrests and trials of leaders of, 101–6
  autonomous status of, 66–68
  Bauhaus architecture of, 66–67, 94
  Bergelson's visits to and promotion of,
    53–71, 93, 95
  book burnings in, 111–12
  celebrations of Bergelson in, 71
  Central Committee resolution of
    1949 on, 98–99
  collective farms of, 47–52, 57, 61, 69,
    98, 130
  contemporary Jewish population of,
    96–97, 99, 113–14, 130, 135–39
  departures of settlers from, 52, 57, 66, 98
  Dubnow's concept of autonomism
    and, 18
  early settlement of, 48–52
  flag of, 131
  Great Terror purges in, 9, 68–71, 94,
    98–100, 107–15, 126, 133–35
  industrial plan for, 57–60
  Jewish emigration to Israel from, 133,
    139, 147
  Jewish settlers of, 7–9, 50–52, 65–66
  Jewish tourist sites in, 129–35
  Jewish World War II refugees and
    orphans in, 72, 93–99, 108, 112,
    134–35, 146

Kazakevich's promotion of, 61–62
Korean population of, 49, 69
Nazi collaborators in, 130–31
post-Stalinist period in, 126–28
Russification policy in, 112–15
Tikhonkaya workers' settlement of,
    50, 52, 56–57
Yiddish conference planned for,
    67–69, 92
Yiddish language and culture in, 6,
    8–10, 60–62, 70–71, 93–95, 107–10,
    126–28, 130, 139, 145–47
Birobidzhan (Miller), 107–8
Birobidzhan, My Home (Vasserman), 127
Birobidzhaner (Bergelson), 63
Birobidzhaner shtern, 60, 65, 70, 108–9,
    113–14, 146–47
The Birobidzhan Generation (Vergelis),
    108
Birobidzhan journal, 95, 111
Birobidzhan Philharmonic, 131
Birobidzhanskaya zveda, 70, 109
Birobidzhan State Archives, 134–35
Birobidzhanstroy, 60
Birofeld farm, 50
The Black Book, 88–90, 100, 124
Brokhin, Zynovy, 109
Brown, David, 57–60
Bumagin, Iosif, 132–33
the Bund, 26, 77, 85

Cahan, Ab, 36–37, 40–42
"Citizen Taiga Has the Floor"
    (E. Kazakevich), 1, 62
Committee for the Settlement of Toiling
    Jews on the Land (OZET), 48–50,
    70, 122–23
Crimean Jewish settlements, 43, 47,
    92–93, 117

"The Dancer from the Ghetto"
    (Markish), 73
Der emes daily, 37–38, 40–41, 84
Der fraynd daily, 62

Der Nister (pseud.), 15, 33, 36, 125
Der tog daily, 45
Dizengoff, Meir, 22
Dubnova-Erlich, Sofia, 26, 77–78, 85
Dubnow, Simon, 18–29, 32, 38
    execution of, 74–76, 144
    on interwar Berlin, 35–36
    on Jewish emigration and self-defense,
        23–27
    on Jewish identity and autonomy,
        19–23, 25–26, 145
    on Jews in the Soviet Union, 39–41
    vision of multipolar Jewish world of,
        27–28
    on World War II, 75–77, 86
    on Yiddish language use, 35
    on Zionism, 20–22, 41

Ehrenburg, Ilya, 80, 89, 93
Eichmann, Adolf, 82
Einstein, Albert, 35, 89–90
emigration
    knowing when to go and, 4, 10–12,
        77–78
    loss of language in, 15–16
    possible destinations for, 5–6, 54–55
    of Soviet Jews, 3–7, 63, 133, 139–44
Emiot, Israel, 94–95, 107–8, 111, 126
Erlich, Henryk, 26, 76, 85
Eynikayt newspaper, 85–86, 88, 116–17
    The Black Book of, 89–90, 100, 124
    closure of, 101

Fefer, Itsik, 92, 111, 114, 116–18, 124–25
Forpost, 67–68, 111
Forverts, 35–37, 40–41, 45, 85
Freiheit daily, 41–42, 45–46
French Revolution, 39
Freud Jewish Community Center, 131,
    136

"Gedenkt" (Bergelson), 86
Goldberg, Ben Zion, 101–2, 104–5, 117
Di Goldgreber (Aleichem), 67

Gorky Park rally, 79–82
Great Terror
    arrests and trials of the JAC in,
        100–106
    in Birobidzhan, 9, 68–71, 94, 98–100,
        107–15, 126, 133–35
    Night of the Murdered Poets of, 12,
        124–25
    purges of Yiddish writings in, 111–15,
        133
    Russification policies of, 112–15
Gurevich, Valery, 131, 138–39

Ha-Am, Ahad, 19
Hebrew language use, 13, 16–17
    by Dubnow, 18
    in Palestine/Israel, 41, 147
    Soviet banning of, 5–6, 80
He Is from Birobidzhan (Miller), 108
Herzl, Theodor, 21
"A Historic Moment (The Question of
    Emigration)" (Dubnow), 22–23
Hitler, Adolf, 54
Hofshteyn, Dovid, 15, 31, 116, 125
the Holocaust, 9, 28, 73–77, 82
    Bergelson's writing on, 73–74, 85–90
    The Black Book of, 89–90, 100, 124
    death camps of, 88–89
    local massacres of Jews in, 74–75,
        83–84, 87, 96
    Rumbula Forest monument of, 142–44
    Soviet Jews lost in, 91
    Soviet narratives of, 134–35, 142–43
    survivors of, 91–99

Ignatyev, Semyon, 100–106
IKOR farm, 51
In Search of Happiness, 137
In shpan journal, 41–42
Israel, 90, 127–28
    emigration of Soviet Jews to, 63, 133,
        139–44, 147
    Soviet diplomatic relations with, 141,
        146–47

Jabotinsky, Vladimir (Ze'ev), 22–23
Jewish Anti-Fascist Committee (JAC),
    85–87, 89–93
    American support of, 92, 103–4
    Eynikayt newspaper of, 85–86, 88–90,
        100–101, 116–17
    Great Terror purge of, 100–106, 123–25
Jewish Autonomous Region, 8–9
    museum accounts of history of, 132–35
    official establishment of, 66–68
    remaining Jewish population in,
        96–97, 99, 113–14, 130, 135–39
    seventy-fifth anniversary of, 129
    See also Birobidzhan
Jewish Chamber Theater, 131
Jewish enlightenment movement, 13
Jewish identity, 7–11, 143–48
    Dubnow's views on, 19–29, 39–41
    Great Terror attacks on, 68–71, 94,
        100–125
    knowing when to run and, 4, 10–12,
        77–78
    Soviet policies on, 37, 39–42, 90
    Yiddish literary scene and, 13–17
    See also anti-Semitism
The Jewish State (Herzl), 21

Kaganovich, Lazar, 67–70, 92–93
Kaganovich State Jewish Theater,
    67–68, 71
Kalinin, Mikhail, 47–48
Kazakevich, Emmanuil, 60–62, 71
    flight from Birobidzhan of, 69, 94
    theater of, 66–69
Kazakevich, Henekh, 60
Khavkin, Marvei, 64–70, 92–93
Khavkin, Sofia, 70, 92–93
Khazansky, Matvey, 93–94
Khrushchev, Nikita, 135
Kh'vel lebn (Bergelson), 83, 91
Kishinev pogrom, 22–23, 27
knowing when to run, 4, 10–12, 77–78
Kogan, Anna, 112–13
Kogan, Sima, 69–70

Komarov, Vladimir, 102
KOMZET, 70
Korn, Rokhl, 87–88
Kristallnacht, 26–27
Kulture-Lige, 31–32, 119
Kushnir, Savely, 109
Kvitko, Leyb, 15, 31, 33, 36, 79, 85
    Great Terror and, 103, 116, 125
    mission to Crimea of, 92–93, 103
Kyiv, 119–20
    Bergelson's homage to, 86–88
    German massacres of Jews of,
        83–84, 87
    Yiddish language and culture in,
        14–15, 30–31, 87, 101, 120–21
Kyiv Group, 14–15, 31

Labor Zionism, 13, 15
League of Nations, 39
Lenin, Vladimir, 129
Letters on Old and New Judaism
    (Dubnow), 18
Levitin, Mikhail, 108–9
LGTB families, 11
Liberberg, Joseph, 64, 67–70
Litvakov, Moyshe, 34–35, 38, 43, 67–68,
    109, 119
Lozovsky, Solomon, 79, 116

Majdanek death camp, 88–89
Makhno, Nestor, 29
Markish, Perets, 31–32, 36, 79
    on Bergelson's prosperity, 64
    Great Terror and, 111, 116–18, 125
    Soviet propaganda by, 73
    on Yiddish literature, 34–35
Matrosov, Alexander, 132–33
"May the World Be a Witness"
    (Bergelson), 85–86
Mendelevich, Yosef, 142–44
Meyer, Hannes, 66–67
Mikhoels, Solomon, 67, 79–80, 85, 137
    JAC fundraising trip of, 92
    murder of, 100–101

Miller, Buzi, 107–9, 111, 114
Molotov-Ribbentrop Pact, 72–74

Night of the Murdered Poets, 12, 124–25

OZET. *See* Committee for the Settlement of Toiling Jews on the Land

Pale of Settlement, 9, 47, 61, 97, 132
    Bund movement in, 26, 77, 85
    Jewish enlightenment movement in, 12–13
    Kyiv Group of, 14–15, 31
    local massacres of Jews in, 74–75, 83–84, 87, 96
    pogroms in, 12
Palestine, 45–46, 54–55, 90
    See also Israel; Zionism
Palestinian Communist Party, 46
Petlyura, Symon, 29
Poland, 25–26
    See also Pale of Settlement
Prints Ruveni (Bergelson), 91
Putin, Vladimir, 75

Rak, Maria, 130–31, 139
"The Red Army Soldier" (Bergelson), 44
Reed, John, 37
Rehabilitation Through Training movement, 35
Romanisches Café, 34, 43, 46
Rumbula Forest massacre, 74–75, 142–44
Russian language use, 17, 33
    by Dubnow, 18
    in Russified Birobidzhan, 112–15
Russian Revolution of 1905, 23, 39
Russian Revolution of 1917, 23–24, 29–30, 39, 119–20
Russification programs, 112–15

Salisbury, Harrison, 126
secular Judaism, 18–20
Shkolnik, Leonid, 145–47
Shkolnik, Leyba, 52

Sholem Aleichem Club, 35
Sholem Aleichem Library, 112, 126, 129–30, 145–46
Shtern, Lina, 105–6, 124, 125
Simchat Torah, 136
Singalovsky, Aaron, 35
Slutsky, Ber, 108
Stalinist terror. *See* Great Terror
Sunrise (Emiot), 111
Suslof, Mikhail, 100
"Symphony" (Emiot), 107
Syrkin, Nachman, 13

Tchernovitz-Avidar, Yemima, 127–28, 146
Temnorod, Izya, 112–13
Temnorod, Motya (Dmitry), 113
Ten Days That Shook the World (Reed), 37
Teploye Ozero settlement, 113–14
Territorialism, 15
Tikhonkaya workers' settlement, 50, 52, 56–57
Trevoga farm, 69
Tribuna journal, 70
Two Five-Year Plans, 64

Ukraine
    Bolshevik government of, 31–32
    Kulture-Lige of, 31–32, 119
    Kyiv Group of, 14–15, 31
    laws on autonomous minority governments in, 30–31
    See also Pale of Settlement
Ulinich, Anya, 16
"An Unusual Ending" (Bergelson), 37

Valdheym farm, 51–52, 61, 130
Vapnyar, Lara, 16
Vasserman, Lyubov, 130, 133
    Great Terror purges and, 108–9, 111, 114–15
    promotion of Yiddish writing by, 95, 127
Vayserman, David, 135
Victory Day, 91

When All Is Said and Done (Bergelson), 44
White Army, 29–30
World War II
    Jewish orphans from, 93–94, 108, 112
    Jewish refugees from, 72–73, 91–99,
        134–35, 146
    Jewish support of the Soviet war
        effort of, 79–91
    Nazi collaborators from, 130–31
    occupied Baltic states of, 72, 74–78
    official Soviet histories of, 123–24,
        132–33
    See also the Holocaust

Yarmitsky, Abram, 109
Yeltsin, Boris, 133
Yevsektsia, 32–35, 67–68
    Bergelson's attacks on, 37
    Der emes daily of, 37–38, 40–41, 84
Yiddish language and culture, 13–17
    Bergelson's advocacy for, 31–36, 41–42,
        65–71, 84

in Birobidzhan, 6, 8–10, 60–62,
    70–71, 93–95, 107–10, 126–28, 130,
    139, 145–47
Dubnow on, 35
Great Terror purges and, 68–71, 94,
    101–25, 133–35
in interwar Berlin, 33–37, 121
in Kyiv, 14–15, 30–31, 120–21
in New York, 35–37, 40–42
in the Pale of Settlement, 12–13, 132
Soviet support of, 34–35, 73
Ukraine's Kulture-Lige and, 31–32, 119
YIVO (Institute for Jewish Research),
    26, 76

Zionism
    Dubnow's views on, 20–22, 41
    Hebrew language campaign and, 41
    Soviet policies against, 5, 41, 43, 46,
        90, 100
    See also Israel; Palestine
Zuskin, Benjamin, 137

ABOUT THE AUTHOR

Masha Gessen is a Russian-American journalist who is the author of several books, including *The Brothers: The Road to an American Tragedy* and the national best seller *The Man Without a Face: The Unlikely Rise of Vladimir Putin.* Her work has appears in *The New Yorker, The New York Times, The New York Review of Books,* and many other publications. She has received numerous awards, including the 2015 Raoul Wallenberg Medal from the University of Michigan and a 2015–16 Carnegie Millennial Fellowship. She lives in New York City.

RUSSIA'S JEWISH AUTONOMOUS REGION

90°F
60°F
30°F
0°F
-30°F

J F M A M J J A S O N D
Birobidzhan

TYPE OF LANDS IN 1931

Forested mountains

Other
Utilized lands

Swamps

Forest, bush

Birobidzhan
14,800 mi²
205 miles

CHANGE OVER TIME: NUMBER OF JEWS IN THE POPULATION OF

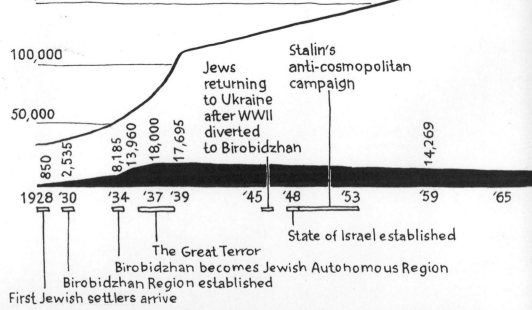

150,000

100,000

Jews returning to Ukraine after WWII diverted to Birobidzhan

Stalin's anti-cosmopolitan campaign

50,000

850   2,535   8,185   13,960   18,000   17,695   14,269

1928 '30   '34   '37 '39   '45 '48   '53   '59   '65

State of Israel established

The Great Terror
Birobidzhan becomes Jewish Autohomous Region
Birobidzhan Region established
First Jewish settlers arrive